ATOMIC DAWN

A People in Focus Book

ATOMIC DAWN

A BIOGRAPHY OF
ROBERT OPPENHEIMER

BY J. E. DRIEMEN

ᴅP DILLON PRESS, INC.
Minneapolis, Minnesota 55415

Photographic Acknowledgments

The photographs are reproduced through the courtesy of Argonne National Laboratory; Bulletin of the Atomic Scientists; Harvard University Archives; J. Robert Oppenheimer Memorial Committee; Los Alamos National Laboratory; United Nations; and University Archivist, the Bancroft Library, University of California, Berkeley.

Library of Congress Cataloging-in-Publication Data

Driemen, J. E.
Atomic dawn : a biography of Robert Oppenheimer / by J. E. Driemen.
(A People in focus book)
Bibliography: p.
Includes index.
ISBN 0-87518-397-2

1. Oppenheimer, J. Robert, 1904-1967—Juvenile literature.
2. Atomic bomb—United States—History—Juvenile literature.
3. Physicists—United States—Biography—Juvenile literature.
I. Title. II. Series.
QC16.062D75   1989
530'.092'4—dc 19
[B]   88-18968
                                                                  CIP

Dillon Press, Inc., 242 Portland Avenue South
Minneapolis, Minnesota 55415

Printed in the United States of America
1 2 3 4 5 6 7 8 9 10 98 97 96 95 94 93 92 91 90 89

Contents

Chapter / One

The Blast Heard around the World

Just before dawn, on the morning of July 16, 1945, in a remote area of New Mexico, the earth shook violently, and the darkness lit up with a sudden blaze of blinding light. It was as if the sun, instead of creeping over the horizon and rising gradually into the heavens, had made a giant leap into the middle of the sky. The light was so intense that the human eye could not stand to look at it.

The explosion had come from a desert area that was used as a practice bombing range by the United States Army in World War II. Known as the White Sands Missile Range, it also had a much older name, given to it by the Spanish explorers 400 years earlier: Jornada del Muerto, or "Journey of Death."

One hundred and twenty miles northwest of

The first atomic explosion lit up the test site in the New Mexico desert.

the site, the explosion shook the city of Albuquerque. Tremors were also felt further north in Santa
Fe. There the people linked the event to the secret
military activity that had been going on for two
years in a nearby place called Los Alamos. But the
huge size and power of this blast was far greater
than could be explained by practice bombing. The
shock could even be felt more than 200 miles to the
south in El Paso, Texas.

Actually, this was a nuclear explosion—the first
one ever created by human beings. The bomb that
produced the explosion had been built in great
secrecy at Los Alamos. And the person who, more
than anyone else, made it work was the famous
physicist, J. Robert Oppenheimer. Later, *Time* magazine would call him "the father of the atomic
bomb."

For those who were there, that first test was a
time of extreme suspense. Three separate observation stations were set up to watch it. These were
arranged to the north, east, and west; each was
located about six miles from Ground Zero. The
observers included the scientists and technicians
who had worked with Oppenheimer on the bomb,
many high-ranking government and military leaders, and a large group of army personnel assigned to
the project. They were warned not to look directly

Robert Oppenheimer.

at the blast, even with special dark glass shields. One man ignored the warning. He went blind.

Some scientists worried that the nuclear explosion might ignite the atmosphere and set fire to the whole planet Earth. That did not happen, but the first bomb changed the world forever in ways that have not yet been fully measured. In that atomic dawn, the nuclear age had begun.

U.S. scientists and leaders had created the bomb because they feared Nazi Germany might make one first. That would make it the strongest military power in the world. The Allies in Europe— England and France—had been at war with the Axis powers—Germany and Italy—since September 1939. The United States declared war against both Germany and Japan immediately after the surprise attack by Japan against the U.S. Navy base at Pearl Harbor, Hawaii, on December 7, 1941. As the war went on, the United States and its allies launched a very large, but secret, project to make the first atomic bomb.

To build such a bomb meant finding a way to turn the theory of nuclear fission—the splitting of an atom—into a practical military weapon that could be controlled by people. This was the task that was given to Robert Oppenheimer—a task that he accomplished brilliantly.

He did not do it alone. It required a tremendous effort by hundreds of physicists, chemists, and engineers who came together in one of the most dramatic examples of teamwork in human history. To call Oppenheimer the father of the bomb may have been an exaggeration. He was more of a leader, a coach, a team captain rather than an individual inventor. But he was the one who brought together the ideas of the many scientists, and who made them fit and made them work. He was a national hero.

Yet there was also a dark side to the creation of the bomb. When they had a chance to think about it, many of the scientists began to regret what they had accomplished. Oppenheimer shared their fears. The destructive power of atomic bombs was greater than anyone had expected.

The scientists' concern did not stop the building of more and bigger bombs. When the Soviet Union also learned to make them, a nuclear arms race began. These events affected Oppenheimer in a special way. Only nine years after the end of the war, some U.S. government officials accused him of being a traitor. During the war he had been trusted with the most sensitive secrets of the U.S. military. His loyalty and patriotism had never been questioned. But now it was rumored that he had betrayed his country by sharing the atomic knowledge he had helped develop with the Communist government of the Soviet Union.

Oppenheimer was never actually charged with treason or brought to trial. Yet, as a result of a hearing before the members of the Atomic Energy Commission, his security clearance was cancelled. That meant he could no longer work for the U.S. government or share in any information that resulted from government research into nuclear science.

No one, not even his enemies, questioned his scientific brilliance. The political and military leaders of the day almost unanimously declared that the atomic bomb project could not have succeeded without his leadership. Oppenheimer continued to study and teach for more than twelve years after the hearings, until his death in February 1967. Still, he never regained his security clearance or the unquestioned trust and respect of the American people.

How, then, could a man who played such a giant part in modern history go from being a national hero to a suspected traitor in just nine years? The answer to that question is the story of J. Robert Oppenheimer, one of the most brilliant physicists of the twentieth century.

Chapter/Two

Too Good to be True

The Oppenheimer family had its roots in Germany, in the city of Hanau. The first members of the family to come to the United States were two cousins of Robert's grandfather, Ben. In 1870 the cousins arrived in New York City, where they set up a business importing cloth from England and Germany for the growing American clothing industry. The two men prospered, and in 1888 they invited Ben's seventeen-year-old son Julius to join them in New York. They promised young Julius a job and a future.

He began work in the storeroom, doing the simple tasks of unpacking, sorting, and stacking bolts of cloth. He also had to keep an inventory, a list of everything in stock. This humble beginning was part of a tradition that a newcomer must start at the bottom to learn the business. It was also necessary because Julius spoke almost no English. This was work he could do without knowing the language of his new country.

But Julius was not only bright and ambitious; he believed enthusiastically in self-improvement. He made it a point to learn English quickly, and well. He also read a great deal and taught himself in many subjects such as science, music, and the arts.

Like his older cousins, Julius prospered. By the time he was thirty, he was a successful, highly respected merchant, also in the importing business. His interest in the arts probably led to his meeting a young woman named Ella Friedman at an exhibit of paintings in a museum.

Like Julius, Ella was of European-Jewish descent. But unlike him, she, as well as her parents, had been born in the United States. People said she was beautiful, though she had a slightly deformed right hand and always wore long gloves to hide it. Ella became a well-known artist, and she also taught painting in her own studio.

Early in 1903, Ella Friedman and Julius Oppenheimer were married. On April 22, 1904, their first child, Robert, was born. The J (for Julius) was added to Robert's name as an afterthought to make

Julius and Robert Oppenheimer. Robert is about two years old in this picture.

it more impressive. Two other sons were born to the Oppenheimers. The second child died in infancy, and the third son, Frank, was born in 1912.

The story of Robert's childhood is a simple one. While his parents were not wealthy, they had enough money to live comfortably. The young child enjoyed all the benefits and comforts of a well-to-do family. His parents gave him so much love and attention that they nearly spoiled him. When he was five, he traveled with them to Germany to visit the Oppenheimers' ancestral home. His grandfather, Ben, who never came to the United States, gave him a small collection of rocks and minerals.

Young Robert with his mother, Ella Oppenheimer.

Mineralogy became the youngster's first hobby. With almost no friends or playmates, he would spend hours collecting, polishing, and cataloging rock samples. He pursued this hobby so intensely that he was invited to become a member of the New York Mineralogical Society when he was only eleven. At twelve, he presented his first scientific paper—on minerals—to this society of adult mineral experts. Of his own childhood he later wrote, "I was an abnormally, repulsively good little boy." What he probably meant was that he was "too good to be true."

Robert did not attend public schools. While his

parents never hid the fact that they were Jewish, they did not practice the Jewish religion or follow Jewish social custom and tradition. Robert was sent to a private school connected with the New York Society of Ethical Culture.

The curriculum, or program, of this school included all the subjects common to private schools of that time: Greek, Latin, mathematics, chemistry, literature, and so on. But it also promoted the idea that the kinds of values and morals people associate with religion could be practiced without a person's belonging to a recognized church or synagogue.

Robert was an outstanding student. If anything, he worked too hard at his studies. He had no skills in most sports and seemed to dislike any heavy physical activity. In fact, he would not use the stairs at his school; instead, he would wait for the elevator. School officials were finally forced to send a note to his parents. It read: "Please teach your son to walk up the stairs. He is holding up classes." Robert tried playing tennis but played so poorly that he soon quit. He refused to try anything he felt he could not do well.

As Robert grew older, he did become skilled at one sport—sailing. The family had a summer home on Long Island, New York, facing the Atlantic Ocean. When Robert was eighteen, his father gave him a twenty-eight-foot sailing craft. Robert named it *Trimethy*—probably after the chemical element, trimethylene oxide—and he and his brother spent hours sailing it. Once, a storm took them far out to sea. A coast guard cutter went out to look for the two boys. Cut off from all communication, they spent five hours working the craft back into the shelter of the bay near their summer home. They made it to safety on their own, and their relieved parents did not even scold them for their recklessness.

As a teenager, Robert mostly kept to himself. Although he is remembered as being very polite and correct in every way with adults and peers, he was also considered a "brainy snob." He never hid his scorn for those he felt were not as smart, and he spent much of his time reading books. That kind of behavior didn't make him very popular with his schoolmates. At a summer camp when he was fourteen, some of his fellow campers, who were fed up with his display of highbrow superiority, locked him up naked in an icehouse overnight.

He took this kind of abuse in stride and did not let it discourage him from his bookish interests. If a new subject caught his fancy, he pursued it with all-out enthusiasm. When, for example, a chemistry instructor at the Ethical Culture School sparked his

Robert (right) at about age twelve with a friend. At this age, "minerals, writing poems and reading, and building with blocks...architecture..." were his favorite activities.

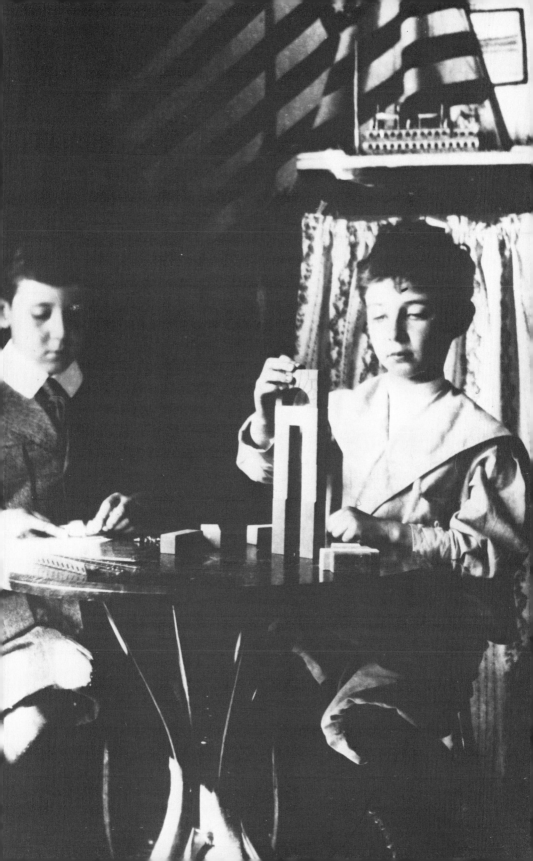

interest in science, Robert spent an entire summer holiday helping the instructor build a laboratory— just for the sheer joy of it and without any thought of being paid.

In his last year at school, Robert concentrated on his studies and finished with perfect marks. Partly as a reward, and partly because he was mentally and physically exhausted, his parents took him overseas with them to visit Germany again. Robert, now seventeen years old, went off alone into the Harz Mountains to go rock collecting. Typically, he worked too hard at it and developed some serious stomach problems. As a result, he suffered all his life from indigestion.

Robert had been accepted at Harvard and had planned to enter the university that fall. When he returned from Europe, though, he was too sick to attend college. He agreed with his father to stay out of school for that year. During this time he became moody and ill-tempered and would lock himself into his room for days. He did a lot of reading, but his parents had a very difficult time trying to get him to be more sociable.

In the spring of 1922, Julius Oppenheimer called on Robert's high school English teacher and told him about his son's problems. Robert was very fond of this teacher, a young, athletic man named

Herbert Smith. Mr. Smith convinced Robert to come camping with him for the summer in the mountains of Colorado and New Mexico.

The teacher and his former pupil spent the summer exploring the wild country, on foot and on horseback. They established a warm friendship that would continue for the rest of their lives. Sometimes they stayed at high-class ranches, but usually they slept and ate out-of-doors. Robert became a new person. He was tall, over six feet, but extremely thin. Though he remained slender and frail-looking all his life, in the western mountains he developed a physical ruggedness that would serve him well. And in those mountains he discovered a fondness for horses that led him to become an expert rider.

At the Los Piños Ranch near Santa Fe, Robert fell madly in love with Katherine Page, the woman who managed the resort. She was much older than Robert, and nothing came of this teenage love. He fell in love with the high country around Santa Fe, too. The desert and mountains and people of New Mexico attracted him in a powerful and mysterious way.

The joyful summer greatly refreshed young Oppenheimer. In the fall of 1922, he was ready for Harvard. Robert wasn't sure what he wanted to study. He had thought of architecture, and about

being a writer, a poet, and a painter. Still, the pull of science was strong, and he decided to major in chemistry.

Again, he devoted almost all of his time and energy to his studies. For a while he did take an interest in a university literary magazine, contributing some poems and short stories. Yet he took part in almost no social activities and, according to the people who knew him, never went out on a date. He was so wrapped up in his studies that even his eating habits took a curious twist. His favorite meal consisted of what he called a "black and tan" sandwich: a thick layer of peanut butter between two slices of toast, topped with heaps of chocolate sauce. This, he claimed, gave him all the nourishment he needed.

Robert finished the four-year university course in three, graduating with top honors. His major was chemistry, but he was still not sure in what field he wanted to work. During his final year at Harvard, though, he had enrolled in a course in thermodynamics—the use of heat to produce power—taught by a famous physicist, Percy Bridgman.

Oppenheimer fell in love with the science of physics. To him it seemed more philosophical, even more "poetic" than chemistry which, he said, was almost too practical. Professor Bridgman was equal-

This photograph shows Robert Oppenheimer at about the time he graduated from Harvard.

ly impressed with the young student. He did feel
that Oppenheimer was sometimes overeager in trying to impress people with his knowledge and brain-
iness. But he believed Robert had a future in science, particularly in physics.

He recommended the new graduate for a fellowship to do postgraduate study in physics at the
Cavendish Laboratory at Cambridge University in
England. On the basis of this recommendation,
Ernest Rutherford, the director of the laboratory,
accepted the young man's application. The future
physicist had been born.

Chapter/Three

A Small Gamble and a Poisoned Apple

The 1920s, when Robert Oppenheimer traveled to England to do his postgraduate work, were exciting times for science. New discoveries in all branches of science multiplied so swiftly that even scientists found it hard to keep up with them.

This was especially true in physics. Albert Einstein's theories about matter and energy had sparked a revolution in this science. For Einstein, matter referred to all the elements that make up the world as we know it: air, water, earth, the metals, as well as animal (including human) and plant life. Energy referred to how these elements worked, and to the power they contained. These were the mysteries that captured the attention of many of the physicists of that time.

Much of their research was devoted to exploring the secrets of the atom. The atom was then believed to be the smallest building block of all things: animal, vegetable, or mineral. Earlier scientists had shown that all matter was made up of atoms.

According to one theory about the structure of an atom, this tiny building block was like a miniature solar system. Each atom had a central part, or nucleus, like the sun. Surrounding this core were electrons—tiny particles of energy that moved around the nucleus in fixed orbits, just as the planets of the solar system circle the sun. Physicists used this theory, and others, in their efforts to uncover the secrets of the atom.

It was into this boiling kettle of exciting research—in its early stages—that Robert Oppenheimer plunged when he arrived in Cambridge, England, in the late summer of 1925.

He did not get off to a good start. His major in chemistry had not really prepared him for advanced physics. In particular, the mathematics courses he had taken were not nearly as complete as they needed to be.

These, however, were only minor stumbling blocks compared to the type of scientific work Robert had to do at Cavendish Laboratory. At this well-known laboratory, researchers focused on experimental testing of materials and methods related to research in physics. This would prove to be Robert's weakest area as a physicist.

Though he probably did not realize it then, his strongest talent and chief interest would lie in figuring out theories, mentally or on blackboards. He would use his powers of imagination to explore and develop new, unproved scientific ideas. In science, the word for this activity is *analysis*.

When Professor Bridgman of Harvard wrote his letter of recommendation to Sir Ernest Rutherford at Cambridge, he said bluntly: "[Oppenheimer's] type of mind is analytical rather than physical, and he is not at home in the manipulations [the mechanical work] of the laboratory." In the same letter, he also wrote: "It appears to me that it is a bit of a gamble as to whether Oppenheimer will ever make any real contributions of an important character. But if he does make good at all, I believe it will be a very unusual success; and if you are in a position to take a small gamble without too much trouble, I think you will seldom find a more interesting betting proposition."

Robert himself had expressed his fears and uneasiness at the idea of starting in a laboratory, especially since he was so poorly prepared. He agreed to take some courses to make up for the knowledge he lacked. And instead of working directly with Rutherford, he accepted a lesser assignment to work on an experimental project with a Dr. J. J. Thomson, a Nobel Prize winner.

One of Robert's jobs was to laminate, or "glue" together, very thin sheets of various metals to study the action of electrons beamed through these metal "films." The physical task of putting things together with his hands was almost too much for him. As usual, he could not stand being less than excellent.

Working and living in a foreign land, Robert was homesick for the United States and for his family. There were other Americans at Cambridge. He got to know some of them, and the British students were not unfriendly. Yet Robert continued to suffer from his worst faults: his own demanding nature, his impatience, and his inability to hide feelings of superiority over those he felt were not as intelligent as he. In that sense, he himself was largely responsible for his loneliness.

He did have some friends, mostly other students he had known in the United States, such as Francis Fergusson. In a letter to this young man, who was studying at Oxford, another English university, Robert wrote, "I am having a pretty bad time. The lab work is terrible, and I am so bad at it that it is impossible to feel I am learning anything." He talked often of committing suicide. Those who knew him were fearful he might attempt to harm himself, and they tried to distract him from that idea.

For the Christmas holidays that year, Fergusson persuaded Robert to join him in Paris. During a casual conversation in a café, Robert suddenly leaped out of his chair, jumped on his friend, and grabbed him by the throat as if to strangle him. Fergusson was both heavier and stronger than Robert. He was able to fight off his friend and hold him until Robert calmed down.

There had been nothing in the conversation to trigger or explain this sudden violence. Though it did not cause a breakup of the friendship, it made both young men understand that Robert had serious problems and needed help. When he returned to Cambridge, he went to a psychiatrist.

The psychiatrist concluded that Robert suffered from a mental illness now called schizophrenia. It is a condition of the mind where there is a conflict between a person's feelings and his or her reason. Schizophrenia can cause a person to try to escape into an imaginary dream world created in his or her own mind.

In Robert's case this diagnosis seems to have been much too strong. He was moody and depressed, but he was not trying to run away from reality. He continued to work hard at his studies. Still, he demanded perfection from himself, and his work wasn't going nearly as well as he thought it should.

Young Oppenheimer's problems may have been the result of a delayed adolescence—of trying to do too much too soon. He was certainly aware of his own condition. He did, for example, write a letter of apology to Francis Fergusson for trying to attack him. In his letter, he said, "my inability to solder two copper wires together. . .is probably succeeding in getting me crazy."

Later, in the spring of 1926, Fergusson arranged to meet Oppenheimer after what proved to be Robert's final visit to the psychiatrist. "How'd it go?" Francis asked. Robert answered, "He [the doctor] is too stupid to follow me. I know more about my troubles than he does." Fergusson seemed to agree with his friend, and there is no record of other psychiatric visits.

During the spring vacation that year, Oppenheimer joined two other student friends, John Edsall and Jeffries Wyman, for a walking trip across the island of Corsica. Corsica lies in the Mediterranean Sea between the southern coast of France and the western coast of Italy.

The three friends spent ten days hiking through the mountains, staying in small inns or with local farmers. Sometimes they camped outdoors. They had enough money to eat well and enjoy good French wines. They spent hours in lively conversation about physics, French and Russian literature, and a variety of other subjects. The experience sparked a slowly growing cheerfulness in Robert. He began to come out of his depression.

Near the end of their walking tour, John Edsall was arrested by the police for taking pictures of a military fort. When he was taken to a nearby police station for questioning, Robert and Jeffries went along with him. The police did not object to their presence, and they sat outside the office where John was being examined. Through an open door they could clearly hear what was going on. The police were accusing John of being a spy. He was trying to tell them that he was an innocent American tourist, not a spy.

The argument, partly in broken English, partly in French and Italian, amused the two friends listening in the hallway. Jeffries started to laugh, and to his surprise, Robert joined in, laughing uproariously. It was a sign that Robert's dark mood had indeed lifted. The amusement seemed to have an effect on the police, too. They sent the three young Americans on their way with a loud scolding that only increased their laughter.

There was, however, one other strange incident on this trip. The three men had planned to continue their hike through the neighboring island of Sardinia. But on the last evening in Corsica, Robert suddenly announced that he had to return to Cambridge. He had left, he said, a poisoned apple on the desk of Patrick Blackett, a physicist he had been working with at Cavendish Laboratory. He would have to rush back to make sure that Blackett had not eaten the apple. And without further delay, he left for England.

Neither Robert nor anyone else ever explained why he might want to poison a colleague. No poisoned apple was ever found. Years later, Jeffries Wyman had the idea that the "poisoned apple" was a symbol for something else. He, and others, came to believe that it stood for a scientific paper Robert had written, or some notes about research he had been doing. Perhaps in Corsica he had suddenly realized that the paper or research was all wrong. If someone discovered it before he could correct it, it would make him look stupid. In that way it might "poison" his reputation or career.

Despite all the difficulties, Robert continued to work hard, and he did make good progress at Cambridge. In the 1920s, the university attracted many of the world's great scientists, and he had the good fortune to meet and get to know some of them. Among them was Niels Bohr, the Danish physicist who would later win a Nobel Prize. Another physicist, Paul Dirac, developed Bohr's theories about the "solar" structure of atoms into the quantum theory, which established that electrons did not necessarily stay in fixed orbits. This was a revolutionary idea that opened the door for many new discoveries.

Max Born, the director of the Institute of Theoretical Physics at the University of Gottingën in Germany, was one of the respected scientists Robert met at Cambridge. Born was impressed with the young man's brilliance, and not in the least concerned about his personal problems. He invited Robert to join him at Gottingën.

Of that spring of 1926, Robert wrote: "[When I met Born] I forgot about beryllium and films and decided to learn the trade of being a theoretical physicist." He decided to accept Born's invitation. "It just seemed like the next order of business," he wrote. "I felt completely relieved of the responsibility to go back into a laboratory. I hadn't been good. I hadn't done anybody any good, and I hadn't had

any fun whatever; here was something I felt driven
to try."

A miserable year was finally behind him. He
was like a new person, his own best psychiatrist.
Now he knew where he wanted to go.

Chapter/Four

A Brilliant Young Scientist

When Robert Oppenheimer arrived at Gottingën in the fall of 1926, he had already made something of a name for himself. Scientists kept track of each other's work, and the news of someone's outstanding performance spread quickly. Then as now, a kind of science gossip network carried the news. Both the faculty and students at Gottingën knew of Robert's reputation and gave him a warm welcome.

Also, the Journal of the Cambridge Philosophical Society had published two papers Robert had written about quantum physics. What he wrote was not completely original. While scientists do compete with each other, the competition is usually a friendly one. They borrow from each other and build on each other's work. Robert's friend, Paul

Dirac, who developed the quantum theory of the atom, borrowed ideas from a German physicist, Erwin Schrodinger. Robert added still more new ideas to this theory. This is the way scientific knowledge grows.

When Oppenheimer arrived in Gottingën, quantum physics was still in its beginnings. There was no curriculum on the subject, no clear rules. Students and professors met almost as equals to discuss and explore this and other subjects. They shared ideas and argued in a friendly way. Professors listened to students with open minds.

For Robert Oppenheimer, such an open, creative quest for knowledge was an exciting challenge to his brilliance. He couldn't seem to keep his enthusiasm in check, and tended to be a "show-off." Most of the students at Gottingën were no more than two or three years older than twenty-two-year-old Robert. And yet, they began calling him the "child genius" and signed a petition asking the professors to get him to quiet down a little.

Toning down didn't come easily to him. Robert still had no patience with what he considered a lack of intelligence. He was rude to those he felt were mentally slower. Another American student, Ed Condon, said about him, "the trouble is that [Oppenheimer] is so quick on the trigger intellectually that he puts the other guy at a disadvantage. And, darn it, he is always right, or at least right enough."

Robert's expensive clothes and elegant manners also made fellow students uncomfortable. While others had to devote all their efforts to their studies, Robert found time to study Italian so that he could read the poet Dante's great classic, the *Inferno*, in its original language. He mastered Dutch as well, and continued to write poetry himself.

His friend, Paul Dirac, challenged him: "How can you do both—poetry and physics?" Others, too, envied or resented his many different talents. Their comments did not bother him. He went his own way, driven by the strange power of his unusual mind. And curiously, he was highly respected. Even those fellow students who most disliked his highbrow attitude were eager to share his scientific ideas.

Despite the haughty attitude that often offended people, Robert had many likable qualities. He was extremely generous. Anyone who admired something he owned—a shirt, a book, a piece of jewelry—would likely receive that item as a gift. He expected no thanks of any kind in return. Gratitude embarrassed him.

One such gift went to Charlotte Riefenstahl, a physics student at Gottingën. Charlotte and Robert met for the first time on a train returning from a seminar in the city of Hamburg. She had noticed an expensive leather suitcase on the station platform. Among the shabby cases of the other, poorer students, it stood out like a luxurious fur coat among a pile of rags.

When Charlotte asked who owned the suitcase, she was told Robert Oppenheimer. Later, by sheer chance, they happened to sit together on the train. She complimented him on his luggage. The next day, back in Gottingën, he brought the suitcase to her apartment and insisted that she accept it as a gift.

This marked the beginning of an old-fashioned courtship. Robert showered Charlotte with other gifts and took her out on dates as often as possible. He could not do enough for her, and she did not discourage him. After the school year at Gottingën, they continued the courtship back in New York.

The university world in Germany, in which Robert lived and worked, was a special place, full of excitement and good fellowship. The scientists who filled that world relished the joy of working with each other, the thrill and pleasure of a shared voyage of discovery.

Yet outside the academic world was a different Germany, a nation that had been crushed in World

War I. This Germany suffered from frequent unrest and troubled stirrings. The victorious Allies—mainly France and England—had ignored the pleading of the American government to help rebuild the defeated country. Instead, with their own countries also in ruins, they demanded payment for all the terrible damage Germany had caused in four and a half years of bitter conflict.

As a result, the German economy never really recovered from the war. Money had no fixed value. Today a German mark (a unit of currency like the American dollar) is worth between fifty and sixty cents in American money. In 1926, it sometimes took as many as 100 marks to equal one cent! Eventually, people had to carry bushel baskets of paper money—thousands of marks—to buy a loaf of bread. This rapid decline in the value of the German currency was the worst inflation the modern world had ever seen.

There were still some well-to-do people in Germany, but most Germans endured severe hardship. The hard times affected Robert Oppenheimer (and others) in different ways. In Gottingën, for example, he lived in rooms rented in the house of Doctor Cario. The doctor and his family had once been quite prosperous, but inflation had ruined them. To keep their luxurious house, they had to rent rooms to foreign students. In addition to Robert, Paul Dirac also lived in the house for a while.

In these troubled times, bitterness and unrest filled the country. It was in this atmosphere that nazism took root. While not accusing the Carios of Nazi sympathies, Robert wrote to a friend: "The Carios had the typical bitterness on which the Nazi movement rested." In another letter to Francis Fergusson, he wrote that "Jews, Prussians, and French... are severely frowned on."

Robert was Jewish. Although he did not practice the Jewish religion, and the Nazi party was still six years away from taking power, he was disturbed by the growing threat outside the academic world. Many of his relatives still lived in Germany, and he worried about them.

Despite the surrounding shadows, Oppenheimer's enthusiasm for his studies never wavered. He wrote many papers, some with Max Born, about the behavior of atomic particles. In the spring of 1927, he received his Ph.D., or doctorate, from the University of Gottingën.

His reputation continued to grow. Universities in both the United States and Europe tried to hire him for their teaching staffs, much like American universities today recruit promising star athletes. Professor Bridgeman, who had originally recom-

mended Robert to the Cavendish Laboratory at
Cambridge, offered him a postdoctoral fellowship
at Harvard. This was a prized scholarship from the
National Research Council, funded by the Rocke-
feller Foundation, and Robert accepted the offer.

Back in New York in September 1927, he continued his romance with Charlotte Riefenstahl. She
had returned from Europe to take a teaching position at Vassar, a well-known women's college near
New York City. Charlotte had sailed from Europe
with some friends, and Robert met them all when
their boat docked. In a chauffeur-driven limousine,
he took them to the hotel he had chosen for them,
and then to a very fancy restaurant for dinner. He
really wanted to impress Charlotte.

She stayed on in the city for a short while. They
dated almost every day, going to concerts, mu-
seums, and expensive restaurants. Robert brought
her to meet his parents. While Charlotte liked Mr.
and Mrs. Oppenheimer and was greatly impressed
by the family residence, she was bothered by the
way Robert's parents fussed over him. To her, they
seemed overprotective, and he appeared overprotective of them. Charlotte thought he was something of a "mama's boy," and not ready for marriage. After that visit, their relationship slowly
faded.

The first half of the school year, Robert pursued his fellowship at Harvard, where he was offered a full-time teaching job. He turned down the
offer from Harvard because he was also offered a
position at the University of California at Berkeley.
The physics department at this university was just
beginning. Robert believed he could be a pioneer
and a leader there. Berkeley officials also arranged
for him to spend the spring term each year at the
California Institute of Technology at Pasadena, near
Los Angeles. Exciting new things were happening in
physics at Caltech, and he wanted to be part of
them. The variety of a year split between two universities appealed to him, too.

The West Coast would alsc be better for his
health. Robert had been having problems in Europe, possibly because of the damp weather, his
heavy work schedule, and his irregular eating habits.
His doctors suspected he might have tuberculosis, a
disease of the lungs. His extremely thin, lanky body
tended to confirm this diagnosis. The doctors recommended that he spend at least the summer in the
dry desert country of New Mexico, to see if that
climate would help him.

Nothing could please Robert more. He loved
the rugged beauty and open spaces of New Mexico's
high country. Katherine Page, the woman who ran

the dude ranch at Los Piños, helped him and his younger brother Frank find a log cabin in the Sangre de Cristo ("Blood of Christ") mountains. The mountains were so named by the early Spanish explorers, it is said, because of the way the setting sun turned the snow on the peaks a brilliant red color.

The log cabin was rough and small: two rooms on ground level, and two bedrooms above. It had no running water or toilet. Yet it stood in a flower-filled meadow at the foot of the mountains. For Robert, who loved rough camping, its splendid isolation and its peacefulness were like a bit of paradise. When he learned that the cabin could be rented, he fairly exploded with enthusiasm. "Hot dog!" he shouted.

Katherine Page thought that name was a good one for what the Oppenheimer brothers would call their "ranch." To give it a touch of class, she translated *hot dog* into Spanish: *Perro Caliente*. The name stuck. Several years later, Robert's parents bought the cabin and some of the land around it. It would serve as a vacation home for the rest of his life.

The summer in New Mexico did wonders for Robert's physical and mental health. At the time he felt he needed another year in Europe. He was immediately accepted as a lecturer in physics at the University of Leiden in the Netherlands. Along

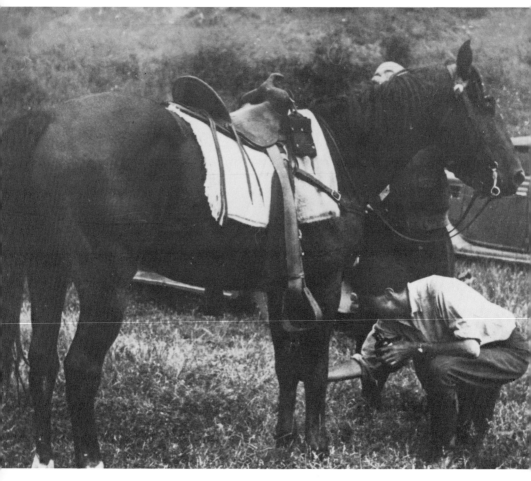

Robert examines his horse, Crisis, at the Perro Caliente ranch in New Mexico's Sangre de Cristo mountains.

with teaching, he studied with the great Dutch physicist, Paul Ehrenfest. When the cold dampness of the Dutch winter at Leiden began to trouble him, he transferred in mid-year to Zurich, Switzerland. There, he worked with another famous scientist, Wolfgang Pauli. He never seemed to have a problem being accepted wherever he wanted to go.

In the summer of 1929, at the age of 25, Robert Oppenheimer returned to the United States to begin his work at Berkeley and at the California Institute of Technology. He would not return to Europe until 1948, three years after the end of World War II.

Chapter/Five

The Oppenheimer "Fan Club"

After a second summer holiday at the Perro Caliente ranch in August 1929, Robert Oppenheimer went up to Berkeley to begin his career as a university professor. At Berkeley, he would be the first to teach theoretical physics. He could also look forward to the spring quarter at Caltech in Pasadena. There the faculty included both theorists—professors concerned mainly with ideas—and others who specialized in laboratory experiments.

At that time, teaching was the only career he considered for himself. He was not interested in experimenting, or in the kind of research that wins Nobel prizes in science. As a teacher, he could play aloud with ideas, and test them out on his students. The classroom would be *his* laboratory. And he would come to know—as many others have discovered—that a good teacher often learns more from teaching than his or her students.

Only advanced graduate students attended his lectures, no more than fifteen or eighteen in a class. Even as a teacher of advanced students, Robert didn't get off to a good start. His mind worked at such high speed that ideas stumbled out almost faster than his mouth could form the right words. His enthusiasm sometimes caused him to stutter, and he had another habit that annoyed almost everyone. When he wanted to emphasize a point, instead of raising his voice as most people do, he would speak so softly that almost no one could hear him.

Even worse for his students was his impatience. He expected everyone to be as quick mentally as he was. If a tough question produced only silence, he was likely to lose his temper. A wrong answer could trigger a storm of anger. More than one student came close to tears as a result of a harsh scolding.

Oppenheimer smoked continuously as he lectured. Students would become so hypnotized by the cigarette in his hand that they would lose track of the lecture. One of them, James Brody, later described his experience in Robert's class. "Since we couldn't understand what he was saying, we watched the cigarette. We [expected] him to write

on the board with it and smoke the chalk. But I
don't think he ever did." Such teaching habits made
it hard for his students to learn—and those were
serious students who intended to make physics
their career.

Many of them complained to the head of the
physics department, Raymond T. Birge. Oppenheimer went too fast, they said. They couldn't follow him, and they couldn't hear.

Robert didn't have to hear these complaints to
know he was doing a poor job. Long before his
students, he had gone to talk to Dr. Birge. He was,
he confessed, a "lousy" teacher. Dr. Birge advised
patience. These young people would not have been
admitted to graduate school if they didn't have
ability, he said. They might not be as brilliant as
their teacher. But if Robert gave them a chance
and took time to get to know them, his classes
might go better.

Oppenheimer determined to try. Yet changing
old habits did not come easily, especially control-
ling his hair-trigger temper. For example, one of his
Gottingën professors, James Franck, on a visit to
Berkeley, attended a lecture by one of Robert's students. In a discussion afterward, Dr. Franck asked a
question not directly related to the subject of the
lecture. Before anyone could answer, Robert burst

out, "That's a foolish question. We'll ignore it."
The class fell silent with embarrassment.

Despite such occasional rudeness, a change had
begun. Robert Serber, another student, said it took
Oppenheimer "five years to mellow." As harsh and
even brutal as the young teacher may have been in
the classroom, with an individual student he could
be the very soul of kindness. When someone came
to him alone with a problem, he would spend hours
patiently going over every detail to make sure the
student understood the problem and could solve it.
These sessions, usually at Robert's living quarters,
sometimes lasted well beyond midnight, interrupted
only when the young professor took time to cook
a meal for both of them.

As he learned to see his pupils as individuals,
to be more patient, they responded with even more
enthusiasm for their studies. Robert, in turn, became even more considerate and caring. His concern for his students did not end with the subject
matter of the course. Although he was not much
older than most of the young people he taught,
he developed a fatherly attitude toward them.

Robert had a wide variety of interests—poetry,
art, philosophy, and literature—and he shared all of
them with his students. He felt he should educate
them not only in physics, but also in the finer things

of life. In Europe he had become an expert gourmet cook, and he shared this skill as well. After a period of eating almost nothing because he was absorbed in a scientific problem, Robert would cook up a great feast for both students and friends. Since he had an inherited income, he could afford to be generous.

And he was generous, in a quiet way. If a student needed financial help, Oppenheimer arranged to slip him some money—without expecting repayment. Often he made a special effort to help a young graduate get a job. He also invited many of his students to spend parts of their summer vacations at the Perro Caliente ranch—at his expense.

Yet it was his brilliance, not his generosity, that turned the majority of class members into what can best be described as a "fan club." Many followed him from Berkeley to Pasadena every spring quarter. Most of them took his courses two and three times just for the excitement of it. In admiration, some imitated the way Robert talked, and the way he walked.

The dramatic change from the terrified students of his early classes to the devoted followers later on caused some resentment among senior faculty members. Dr. Robert Milliken, head of physics at Caltech, frowned on this "bohemian," or arty, independent-minded group. Because of his displeasure,

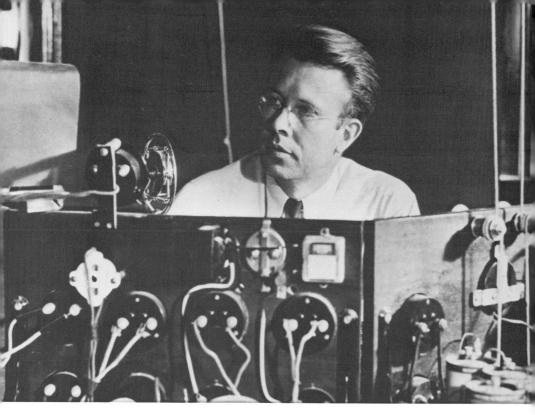

Ernest Lawrence, who invented the cyclotron, was a colleague and friend of Oppenheimer.

on several occasions he blocked the young professor's promotion to a higher academic rank.

Still, no one could dispute Robert's growing success as a teacher. Many of his students became outstanding scientists in their own right. His reputation spread rapidly.

Not everyone in the large physics department at Berkeley resented Oppenheimer's prominence. In fact, some of the other professors were well known themselves. One was Ernest Lawrence, the inventor of the cyclotron, a machine that split atoms to discover how they were put together, and how they worked. He and Robert became close friends.

The two young men had different personalities as well as scientific interests. Lawrence performed experiments, while Oppenheimer worked with theories. Lawrence was jolly and outgoing, and enjoyed sports both as a player and as a spectator. Yet as opposites sometimes do, they were strongly attracted to each other. They shared their scientific ideas, and each contributed in important ways to the other's work.

Despite his passion for teaching physics, Robert did not give up all recreational activity. He loved horseback riding. To his brother Frank he wrote: "I do not have much time for diversions, but I ride at least once a week. There are good horses here and lovely country among the hills surrounding San Francisco Bay."

He enjoyed fast car driving as well. When he moved to Berkeley, his father had given him the old family Chrysler. Sometimes, to relieve the pressures of his work, Robert would race the Chrysler around the mountains of northern California. There were no freeways in those days.

"I take out the Chrysler," he wrote to Frank, "and scare one of my friends out of all sanity by wheeling corners at seventy. The car will do seventy-five without a tremor." It must have been a scary experience to ride with him because, as Rob-

Robert Oppenheimer with Ernest Lawrence (right) *and another scientist at Berkeley.*

ert admitted, "I am and shall [always] be a vile driver."

Frank at that time was attending Johns Hopkins University in Baltimore, Maryland. In his late teens, he often turned to his much admired older brother for advice. Robert cared deeply for his younger brother and felt a serious obligation to help him in every way possible.

In keeping with his own nature, he advised Frank to get as broad an education as possible. "Let me urge you," Robert wrote him, "with every earnestness to keep an open mind, to cultivate. . .an interest in every intellectual discipline, and in the non-academic excellence of the world so that you may not lose that freshness of the mind from which alone the life of the mind derives." Frank majored in biology, but he eventually followed his older brother into physics. It was his own decision.

In October of 1931, Robert and Frank's mother died after a long illness. Herbert Smith, Robert's old high school teacher and camping companion, was with him at the time. He quoted Robert as saying, "I am the loneliest man in the world." He had loved his mother deeply, and it was a time of great sadness for him.

With the help of friends, though, and his dedication to his work, he did not fall into any kind of depression. Also, Robert had always had a good relationship with his father. After his mother's death, his concern for his father's sorrow and loneliness brought the two men even closer together.

Julius Oppenheimer continued to live in New York. Yet at Robert's invitation and insistence, he began to come west regularly, spending weeks at a time with his son both at Berkeley and Pasadena. Robert included his father in as many activities as possible, both social and academic. More than once, Julius attended a lecture, proudly listening to his son even though the subject was a complete mystery to him.

Robert's friends, too, seemed to enjoy Julius. He was lively, interested in many things, and liked talking with the young university students. Even when Robert was busy, his father never lacked the company and the attention of his son's friends. This situation pleased Robert and, in a way, it helped both of them recover from the sorrow of Ella Oppenheimer's death.

As the years went by, Robert gained confidence in himself both as a teacher and as a person. His activities expanded beyond his work in physics. As he matured, his circle of friends grew. He joined the university faculty club and began to spend more time with instructors in other departments. A strong friendship developed between him and Haakon Chevalier, a professor of French. They shared a fondness for poetry, music, and languages. Through Chevalier, too, Robert started to take an interest in politics.

As with other college instructors in the 1930s, Oppenheimer's salary was quite modest. That would hardly have mattered to him. His inheritance, however, paid him $10,000 a year—much more than his salary. Compared to other professors at Berkeley and Caltech, that made him almost rich.

Robert was deeply concerned about the poor pay of many of his colleagues. As he got more and more involved in university business, he took up their cause. He campaigned hard with the administration for higher pay—not for himself but for other instructors. This activity was typical of his widening human interests.

The man who in his growing up years had been looked upon as a self-centered, brainy snob, was now achieving excellence as a theoretical physicist and teacher. But more than that, he was "coming out" of himself, showing more concern for others. More and more people, both outside as well as inside the scientific community, now sought his friendship and company.

Chapter/Six

Politics and Love

The 1930s were a time of great change and unrest, both in the United States and throughout the world. In many European countries, the breakdown of government and industry was producing the conditions that would lead to the outbreak of World War II on September 1, 1939.

Yet at least until 1935, Robert Oppenheimer showed no interest in politics. He paid little attention to what went on in the world outside his scientific field. He didn't read newspapers, he had no radio, and he didn't even have a telephone in his apartment.

When someone challenged him about his lack of interest in national affairs and politics, he said, "What does politics have to do with truth, goodness, or beauty?" These were the qualities he cherished in the science of physics.

During his years at Gottingën, he had been aware of the growing anti-Semitism, or anti-Jewish feelings, in Germany. These changes in German society caused him to worry about his relatives. Still, they did not stir him into political thought or action.

In the late 1920s, the economy of Germany collapsed, and the government seemed helpless to do anything. The Nazi party of Adolf Hitler grew strong. Hitler's private army, the "Brown Shirts," fought in the streets with German Communists. Throughout the country, German citizens were desperate for security and a decent standard of living.

On January 30, 1933, Hitler became the leader of the troubled nation. Once in power, he changed the government from a republic to a dictatorship and ordered attacks against German Jews. These people became the "scapegoats" for the country's problems. It was easy to attack them since they had no way of resisting. Nazi troops either smashed or seized Jewish businesses. Jewish lawyers, doctors, engineers, and others were forbidden to practice their professions. Jewish professors were fired from their jobs.

Robert Oppenheimer was drawn into this situ-

Adolf Hitler (center, front) led the Nazi party to power in Germany during the early 1930s.

ation in two ways. He tried actively to get his relatives out of Germany. He also joined other physicists in setting up an organization to raise money to help Jewish scientists and other teachers escape from that nation, and to help them find positions in the United States or in other democratic countries. He gave freely of his time and money.

This was Robert's first involvement with political causes. Other events spurred him into increased activity. The terrible depression spreading around the world brought hard times to the United States in the 1930s. Factories closed by the thousands, and millions of people lost their jobs. At the worst of

the Great Depression, one out of every four workers was unemployed. Many Americans lost their
homes; they lived in shacks made of tin and card-
board in public parks. And to make things worse, a
terrible drought turned much of the nation's farm-
land into a "dust bowl."

Robert Oppenheimer was not directly affected.
Work at the university went on, and he still enjoyed
enough of an independent income to live comfortably. Bad as things were for one-third of the nation,
the country did not completely collapse. Still, Robert was aware of and troubled by the suffering
around him. Many of his students, for example,
could not get jobs, and some did not have enough
money to live on. He helped out quite a few.

Many of his university friends and other workers began to feel that the American system had
failed. They were attracted by the socialist ideas and
the Communist system of the Soviet Union. After
the Russian Revolution of 1917, Lenin, Stalin, and
other Soviet leaders had set up a system based on
the ideas of Karl Marx.

According to Marx, socialism is a bridge to
communism. Under socialism, the workers would
own and run the factories they worked in. Everyone, wrote Marx, would have a job, a guaranteed
income, and an equal vote in management. Profits

would be divided equally, or according to the importance of each person's contribution. Some private ownership of small business would be allowed.

Communism, Marx wrote, goes a step further. The government would own everything—land, factories, stores, houses, and so on—and would control the use of any profits. Communist party officials would plan all parts of society and take care of all the people's needs. No one would be rich, but no one would be poor.

For many Americans, some kind of "American socialism" promised a solution to the Great Depression that gripped the nation. Factory workers formed unions to demand better treatment and to promote social reforms. Strikes and demonstrations spread across the country. Violence broke out between strikers and police, and occasionally army troops were called on to control riots.

The Soviet Union was used as a model by those who wanted to change American society. Not only unemployed factory workers, but also educated professionals and even farmers were attracted to the idea of socialism. Some of them joined the American Communist party, while others contributed money and support without actually joining. Colleagues and friends of Oppenheimer were numbered among both groups.

These well-intentioned Americans did not know that Soviet communism had become a brutal dictatorship. They did not realize the Soviet people were losing the freedoms that Americans hold dear—personal freedom, the freedom of expression, and the freedom of religion. And they did not see that as much as communism improved living conditions in a once-backward country, it did not deliver all the prosperity it promised.

Though Oppenheimer never became a Communist party member, the events and movements of the times touched him in different ways. In 1936, his brother Frank married a Canadian woman, Jacquenette Quam. She was active in socialist politics and persuaded Frank to join the Communist party with her. Robert did not approve of the marriage (though he later accepted his sister-in-law), nor did he approve of their becoming party members.

Robert was too strong an individual and a free thinker to become a Communist. Yet as more of the people around him became involved in socialist causes and activities, he did support some of them. His good friend, Haakon Chevalier, was one of those who brought him into contact with radical groups.

In 1936, Oppenheimer met Jean Tatlock, a beautiful young woman who was studying for her doctorate in psychology at Berkeley. Her father, John Tatlock, was a professor of literature at that university. He was very conservative in his political beliefs. Perhaps to defy her father, Jean went to the other extreme of actively supporting radical causes. Robert fell in love with her.

More than anyone else, Jean Tatlock brought him into contact with American Communists. Through her influence and his own urge to make a contribution to society, Oppenheimer became involved with a number of organizations: the Consumer's Union, the teacher's union, the American Committee on Democracy and Political Freedom, Friends of the Chinese People, and others. Not all of them were connected with the Communist movement. But the party had a way of getting into any group it thought it could influence. Jean also introduced Robert to several active Communists. One of them was Dr. Thomas Addis, a physician at Stanford University.

Through Addis, Robert became involved with another cause that attracted Communist support in the United States: the Spanish Civil War. After centuries as a monarchy ruled by a king, Spain had become a republic in the 1920s. The country, however, lacked a tradition of democracy and was weakened by the worldwide depression.

In 1936, led by General Francisco Franco, the Spanish military rebelled against the republic it was supposed to defend. Starting in Morocco in North Africa, then a Spanish colony, Franco's troops crossed the Strait of Gibraltar at the western end of the Mediterranean Sea and quickly overran much of the country.

Though they were poorly equipped, many workers and other Spaniards fought back. They were called Loyalists because they were loyal to the established government. For nearly three years, the Loyalists fiercely resisted savage attacks by Franco's forces. They fought in a losing cause.

The Loyalist cause was one of several to which Oppenheimer contributed money—as much as $1,000 per year. He channeled his donations through Jean Tatlock's friend, Dr. Addis, and so through the Communist party. Although he may have intended that the money be spent on medical relief, the funds were probably used to buy military supplies.

His love affair with Jean lasted three years. Robert worshipped her. As in his earlier relationships with women, he showered her with gifts: flowers, jewelry, perfume. It was the wrong thing to do. As a "modern woman," Jean wanted to be treated as an equal, not as an object of worship. She was emotionally disturbed and easily depressed. Jean would disappear for weeks and come back to taunt Robert with stories about other men she had seen. Though she claimed to love him, she seemed to want to hurt him, to bring him down from his "high horse."

Twice they came close to marriage. Their friends said they were miserable when separated, and more miserable together. This tense, unhappy relationship could not last. In 1939, Jean finally decided to end it.

The end of this affair did not cause Robert to stop supporting radical causes. However, he had begun to realize that his work in nuclear physics would probably lead him into military research. Given his position, he wrote much later, "the Communists might have sought to cultivate my friendship in the hope that they could in one way or another take advantage of it." Despite his generous gifts to radical groups, he loved his country and considered himself a patriotic American.

Not long after his breakup with Jean Tatlock, while teaching at Caltech, he met Katherine Puening. Katherine, known as Kitty, was a strong-minded young woman, and a graduate student in biology. She had been born in Germany and had come to the United States at the age of two with her parents. She claimed to be a German princess, and the niece of a famous German military officer, General Keitel.

Though only in her twenties, Kitty had already been married three times. When she and Robert first met, she was married to Dr. Richard Harrison. For Kitty and Robert, it was a case—almost—of "love at first sight." At first, they resisted their feelings for each other. Still, they were drawn together. When Robert invited both the Harrisons to spend a few weeks at the Perro Caliente ranch with the Oppenheimers (including Frank's family), Kitty came alone, without explanations. They decided to get married.

In September 1940, Kitty took up temporary residence in Virginia City, Nevada, so that she could get a divorce in six weeks. On November 1, she was granted a divorce, and she and Robert were married the same day.

Not all of Oppenheimer's friends were pleased with his choice of a wife. Some were troubled by Kitty's three previous marriages and her strong, driving personality. They were concerned that she might lead him away from some of his old academic friends into a more social life style.

Despite these fears, most of his friends were glad to see him settle down. His beloved father Julius had died two years before, and they were

Robert Oppenheimer feeds his son Peter, who was about a year old when this picture was taken.

pleased that Robert would have a family of his own. In May 1941, established in a beautiful new home in San Francisco, Robert and Kitty had their first child, a boy they named Peter.

By this time, Robert was losing interest in radical causes. On December 6, 1941, he attended a reunion for Spanish war veterans. It was the last time he would take part in any such activity. On the very next morning, December 7, Japanese planes attacked the U.S. Navy base at Pearl Harbor. (Germany had already occupied most of Europe.) A day later, President Roosevelt and the U.S. Congress declared war on both Japan and Germany.

"I decided I had had enough of the Spanish cause," Robert wrote to a friend. "There are other more pressing crises in the world." More pressing to him, too, was his growing partnership with his colleague, Ernest Lawrence, in their work on nuclear physics. During the war, Oppenheimer's scientific genius and his ability to explore new ideas with other scientists would thrust him into an immense project that would change the world.

Chapter/Seven

The Manhattan Project

Early in the Second World War, a startling piece of news caught the attention of Robert Oppenheimer and other well-known scientists. Two German physicists, Otto Hahn and Fritz Strassman, had successfully split the uranium atom.

Actually, they were not the first to accomplish such a split. They were, however, the first to do it with the radioactive metal uranium. By bombarding the most common form of natural uranium, U-238, with neutrons, they had extracted U-235, a new isotope, or variety, of uranium that could produce tremendous amounts of power and energy. This process is called fission.

Oppenheimer and other scientists quickly realized that fission could be extended into a nuclear chain reaction. A simple chain reaction can be set in motion by a row of dominos, standing up on end in long rows. Toppling the first domino pushes over the second one, and so on, in a continuing, nonstop chain, until the last domino has fallen. In a nuclear chain reaction, as each atom is split, it releases neutrons that split the next atom, and so on and on. The scientists reasoned that if a chain reaction could be controlled, it could produce heat and electricity. But if the reaction were allowed to run out to a flash point, it could produce a tremendous explosion. In his classes at Berkeley, Oppenheimer began exploring, theoretically and mathematically, what the explosive effects of fission might be.

The German scientists made no effort to keep their discovery a secret. In fact, they published a scientific paper, available to anyone, describing their work. But their government, realizing the paper's possible military use, tried to prevent it from being read in other countries. Another German scientist, Dr. Siegfried Flugge, who did not trust the Nazis, quickly published another article about the possible uses of nuclear energy, and what was going on in his own country. Even in those troubled times, scientists still felt a duty to share openly the discoveries of their research.

Dr. Flugge's article hinted that his government

A portrait of Robert Oppenheimer in the early 1940s.

was trying to keep the results of research secret because it planned to develop a super-bomb, or nuclear explosive, with the uranium atom. At this time there were two major sources of uranium. One was Czechoslovakia, a neighbor of Germany, which the Nazis seized in a bloodless invasion. They maintained strict and complete control over its uranium mines to make sure that no one else could get hold of this valuable metal.

In the United States, Leo Szilard, a Hungarian physicist who had fled from the Nazis, had also been working on nuclear fission. Its potential destructive power frightened him. He pleaded with other American physicists (and those in France and England) to keep their work secret.

When Dr. Flugge's paper was published, it seemed to indicate that German scientists were making rapid progress toward developing a successful bomb. Other scientific "leaks" out of Germany confirmed that the Nazis were pushing hard. Although the United States was not yet directly involved in the war, the danger of the Germans having so powerful a weapon worried Szilard. He felt the American government and military should be warned.

Szilard, an old friend and colleague of Oppenheimer, went into action. He launched a campaign to convince the U.S. government to finance and

Albert Einstein (left) and Leo Szilard review the letter that Einstein sent to President Franklin D. Roosevelt.

support a nuclear research program. Uranium would be needed for such research. In addition to Czechoslovakia, the other major source for this metal was the African land now known as Zaire.

In those days, it was a Belgian colony, the Congo. Szilard knew that Albert Einstein, the famous scientist who had also fled to America from Europe, was a friend of Belgium's King Leopold. In response to Szilard's urging, Einstein persuaded the Belgians to make all their uranium available only to the United States. Also, Einstein wrote a letter to President Franklin Roosevelt proposing that an

American program of research be started.

At first, the president was reluctant to support such a program because he did not think it was a good use of public money. But finally, to an adviser pleading with him to act, he said: "What you are after is to see that the Nazis don't blow us up?" The adviser replied with great emphasis, "Precisely!" The president gave the order, and the program was launched.

It started slowly under the leadership of Vannevar Bush, a prominent scientist from the Carnegie Institute in Pittsburgh. Work on fission was then being done by small teams at universities around the country, and sometimes by single scientists working alone. If they communicated with each other, it was only in a casual, unorganized way. In the summer of 1941, Dr. Bush estimated that it would take at least five years to make a uranium, or plutonium (a heavy, radioactive metal similar chemically to uranium) bomb. He also believed that long before that time, Germany would likely have a nuclear bomb with which to threaten the world.

The war in Europe had been going badly for France and England. In the spring of 1940, the Nazis had "blitzed" Belgium and Holland, captured Paris, and occupied most of France. They had also bombed London and much of England. The English people, led by Winston Churchill, vowed to fight a German invasion, but Hitler had stopped short of invading England.

Instead, in the summer of 1941, he had sent his armies against the Soviet Union. Late in that year, the Germans had driven deep into Russia, to within artillery range of the Soviet capital, Moscow. By then it appeared that the Nazis could conquer all of Europe. The possibility that they might be the first to control the destructive power of the atomic bomb greatly alarmed the Allied nations that fought against them.

While the war raged in Europe, American scientists continued their nuclear research. Dr. Vannever Bush had previously directed Oppenheimer to calculate how much uranium would be needed to start a chain reaction, how fast this reaction had to be, and how much explosive power it could generate.

The theoretical challenge fascinated Robert. He worked out the mathematics—with colleagues and students—in LeConte Hall on the Berkeley campus, where he had his office. Security was tight. All windows were sealed and covered with wire mesh. Only Robert had a key to the room, whose blackboard held many of the secrets of nuclear energy. These calculations were meant to provide the de-

At Berkeley's LeConte Hall, Oppenheimer carried out important research related to nuclear chain reactions.

tailed information engineers would need to design and manufacture an atomic bomb.

Oppenheimer estimated that one kilogram (2.2 pounds) of uranium 235 could produce an explosion equal to five or six tons of dynamite. He also concluded that the most effective bomb would need 100 kilograms (220 pounds) of uranium. The explosive power of this bomb would equal that of thousands of tons of dynamite.

In October 1941, the National Academy of Scientists called a meeting in Schenectady, New York, to discuss the progress of the research. At the request of Ernest Lawrence, Robert attended and presented his findings. His report created much interest, but everyone agreed that there was an urgent need to speed up the program.

Up to this point, work on the project continued to be scattered around the country. A processing plant for refining uranium had been set up at Oak Ridge, Tennessee. At the University of Chicago, under the football stadium, an atomic pile had been built to test a chain reaction. Enrico Fermi, the famous Italian physicist who had also fled from Europe, was in charge. In 1942, a successful nuclear chain reaction was started and shut off as planned. At Berkeley, Ernest Lawrence continued to conduct experiments with electronic magnetism, and scientists at universities in Pittsburgh, Minneapolis, and other places carried out their own research.

Oppenheimer realized that for the huge and complex project to succeed, it would be necessary to bring all the work together in one place. He began to promote the idea in meetings with other scientists. There was another matter to consider as well. By fall 1942, the United States had been officially at war for nine months. With all the difficulties of getting a total war effort organized, the atomic bomb project, important as it was, had not received the attention it needed. Since this was a government project, everyone agreed that an overall boss was needed, a military officer to take charge of the program's non-technical side.

The man chosen for the job was Colonel Leslie R. Groves. Colonel Groves was a West Point graduate, fourth in his class, and an engineer. Earlier in his career, he had been in charge of the construction of the Pentagon, the U.S. military headquarters in Washington, D.C. He had done an excellent job and had won a reputation for getting big jobs done on time, without wasting money. In September 1942, Colonel Groves had command of all military construction in the United States.

Even though he was immediately promoted to brigadier general, his assignment to the atomic bomb project disappointed him. Groves had hoped for a field command, to fight in the front lines of the war. But being a good soldier, he set to work. He named the new assignment the Manhattan Project after his previous command, the Manhattan [New York City] Engineering District.

To begin the new project, Groves visited the major laboratories to make himself familiar with the existing research efforts. He visited laboratories in Pittsburgh, New York City, and Chicago. He was discouraged by the vague answers he received when he questioned scientists about their problems and what they thought could be accomplished.

General Leslie R. Groves was chosen to command the research and development program that became known as the Manhattan Project.

From Chicago Groves went to Berkeley to visit
Ernest Lawrence's radiation laboratory. In contrast
to the other scientists, Lawrence was open, enthusiastic, and down to earth. Still, Groves was disappointed that even Lawrence could not supply him
with the hard facts the general wanted—how long it
would take to get practical results, and what was
needed to make an atomic bomb.

Immediately following his interviews with Lawrence, General Groves went on to meet Oppenheimer. Robert was now devoting himself totally
to nuclear research. He had also discovered a great
sense of pleasure in bringing people together, in
leading them, and in making use of their ideas to
solve scientific problems. The project had become
very important to him.

General Groves quickly sensed that this scientist had special qualities and a strong commitment
to his work. Also, Oppenheimer was the first scientist he had met who could make complicated and
highly technical information understandable to him,
and present the technical choices clearly. The general was so impressed that a week later, he had Oppenheimer join him in Chicago for a train ride back
to New York City to discuss Robert's ideas for a
central laboratory.

In a small, locked compartment, or room, on

the famous Twentieth Century Limited train, Oppenheimer, Groves, and two of the general's aides stayed up all night discussing plans. Robert believed that if all the major scientists needed for the job could be brought together in one place, it would not only make things more efficient, but would also be better for morale. Everyone would know the purpose of the project and would be part of the team, said Oppenheimer. And, if a central laboratory were established in the right place, security would be much easier to maintain for the top-secret project.

Groves especially liked the emphasis on security. Having all the scientists together would keep them focused on the main project. It would be more practical and less costly. To direct the central laboratory, Groves first thought of Ernest Lawrence. Other officials decided that it was more important for Lawrence to continue work with his cyclotron. Groves then chose Robert Oppenheimer as the director.

For all government positions, then and now, a security check of the person chosen is made by the Federal Bureau of Investigation (FBI). For a job as critical as wartime director of atomic bomb development, it was even more important. The FBI had a complete record on Oppenheimer, including his involvement with the Spanish Loyalists and with friends who were Communists or Communist sympathizers. Robert never denied any of this. In fact, he had freely given the FBI much of the information it had in its files about him.

The FBI tried to discourage Groves from naming Oppenheimer as director. The general read all the files. Yet after many serious talks with Robert, he decided—with a "gut feeling"—that this man was a loyal American, as well as being the best qualified for the job.

Groves had the appointment confirmed in Washington, D.C., and made official. Oppenheimer would soon set forth on the most important task of his life.

Chapter/Eight

Leader at Los Alamos

The leaders of the Manhattan Project spent a lot of time trying to decide where to locate the atomic bomb laboratory. It was a difficult and important decision. For example, General Groves ruled out the Oak Ridge plant in Tennessee where uranium was processed because he felt that too much activity in one spot might be an invitation to sabotage.

The project's search group also considered the University of Chicago, site of the first atomic pile and the first chain reaction. That location was ruled out because the scientists worried about an accidental explosion and the damage it might cause. They didn't want to take a chance on blowing up a crowded city. Also, if the laboratory were near a big city, where people could move about freely and come and go as they pleased, it would be hard to keep the project a secret.

Oppenheimer convinced Groves that the laboratory should be in an isolated area. He argued that if all the different experts working on the project came together in some remote place, the quick and easy exchange of ideas would speed up the work. And if the staff was cut off from big cities, they would concentrate more completely on their assignments.

The search group had to consider another problem. Eventually, the bomb would have to be tested in an actual explosion. The test site would have to be close enough to the laboratory to be convenient, yet far enough away from population centers to endanger as few people as possible—from both the explosion and radioactive fallout.

Robert suggested that the search group consider the desert of the American Southwest. This area appeared to meet all the requirements. The U.S. Army already owned a large stretch of land in New Mexico, the White Sands Missile Range, about 160 miles south of Albuquerque. The army used the range for testing big artillery guns. Later in the war, it would also be used by the U.S. Air Force for practice aerial bombing.

In November 1942, Oppenheimer joined

Groves and the general's aide, Colonel John Dud-
ley, in scouting for a location. Near a small settle-
ment called Los Alamos, just a few miles west of the
city of Santa Fe, they found what they were looking
for. On a plateau, a stretch of flat land surrounded
by deep canyons, stood a private school for boys. It
included a number of classrooms, dormitories, and
service buildings, and it had electricity. None of this
was enough even for the limited staff that Robert
thought would be needed. But it would give them a
place where a small group could get started and
where they could build as they grew.

The desert site was wild and beautiful. That
would help make up for the isolation and loneliness
people would experience there. Also, the school
was close enough to both Santa Fe and Albuquerque to be well serviced by railroad and airline transportation. Oppenheimer was delighted by the
choice of Los Alamos. This was like a homecoming
for him. His second home and favorite hideaway,
the Perro Caliente ranch, was only 60 miles away.

General Groves flew to Washington, D.C. With
typical determination, he persuaded the government to buy the Los Alamos Ranch School and
9,000 acres of land—about twelve square miles—
for $415,000. The extra land proved to be a wise
purchase. Oppenheimer had expected to need about

thirty scientists and several hundred support workers for the assignment. Eventually, Los Alamos
grew to be a small city of 6,500.

Before the site could be used, a great deal of
work had to be done. The road from Santa Fe was
so bad that in many places engineers had to build a
new one on top of it. Extra power lines had to be
constructed, along with a much larger system for a
water supply to serve both the growing population
and the laboratory. Thousands of army engineers
struggled through the winter of 1942/43 to build
the camp. General Groves drove the construction
crew hard to get the huge job done on time. He
succeeded.

Oppenheimer directed the plans for the laboratory and the organization of the project. He was
responsible for recruiting the scientists and the
technicians to perform the research and make the
bomb. Groves proposed that all the scientists be
commissioned as officers in the army—lieutenants,
captains, and majors, according to their importance.

After discussing this proposal with the scientists he wanted to work with at Los Alamos, Oppenheimer convinced the general to drop the plan.
There would be plenty of army personnel, Robert
said, for construction, for maintenance, and for
guard duty. But the scientific part of the Manhattan

Project—the making of the atomic bomb—would be a civilian operation. Groves continued in overall command. Robert reported to the general, but he remained in complete charge of the research and manufacturing teams.

Just as he had been when he started teaching, Robert was unsure of himself when he faced the immensely difficult task of organizing Los Alamos. He didn't depend on himself alone for answers. Before he made decisions, he sought advice from many people with more experience than he had. I. I. Rabi, who had been a friend in Europe, and who would later win a Nobel Prize in physics, helped him greatly with wise counsel. Robert Bacher, a former classmate, also served as an advisor.

With a former student, Robert Serber, the director established a plan. Los Alamos would have four main departments: theoretical physics; experimental physics; chemistry and metallurgy (to explore the kind of metals needed for the bomb); and ordnance, or explosives. Originally, the plan called for between 30 and 100 scientists. As the project grew in size and scope, about 1,500 physicists, chemists, engineers, and other technicians came to work at Los Alamos.

To recruit the best scientists, Oppenheimer cleverly started out by persuading several famous physicists to come as the "first team." He reasoned that their reputations would attract others. They came from many countries. From Italy, there were Enrico Fermi, Bruno Rossi, and Emilio Segre. From Hungary came Edward Teller and John von Neumann. Niels Bohr and his son Aage came from Denmark. Victor Weisskopf was from Austria, and Stanislaus Ulan from Poland. Hans Bethe and Rolf Lanshoff were German refugees. George Kistiakowsky had come to the United States from Russia as a teenager.

A few of these scientists were already Nobel Prize winners. Others would win this great honor in the future. This was not only an "all-star" team; it was also an "all-world" team. A number of them were Jewish scientists who had fled to America to escape and fight the Nazis. But they were not a majority, even among the other Europeans who had also rejected the Nazis. Most of the staff of 1,500 were Americans, and many had been Robert's students.

Another group played a big part in the project. The British had also been working on nuclear fission. Scientists from both nations were in constant touch with each other. Yet it soon became clear that Great Britain didn't have the resources to develop a successful bomb on its own. Rather than try to

Enrico Fermi was one of the famous physicists recruited by Oppenheimer as the "first team" for the Manhattan Project.

coordinate a combined effort by both nations, Winston Churchill, the English prime minister, agreed to send British scientists to the United States to work directly with the Americans. Unlike the U.S. scientists, no member of the British group was required to take a security test.

The success that Oppenheimer had in recruiting was remarkable considering what he offered. All he promised was hard work and low pay in a place almost no one had ever heard of. Everyone would have to live and work in a remote wilderness under crude and difficult conditions. Only married scientists in the top rank were allowed to bring their families. Single people had to come alone and promise to cut off their connections to the outside world.

Also, Oppenheimer could tell them they would be engaged in "war work," but nothing more. Only after every scientist had been cleared by security, had accepted a contract, and had settled in at the camp, was Robert allowed to tell them they would have a part in making an atomic bomb.

Officially, even the name Los Alamos did not exist. Its citizens could write and receive letters, but could not mention anything about their work. Outgoing letters used a post office box number in Santa Fe as the return address. Incoming letters had to be

Robert Oppenheimer with Dorothy McKibbin (left), who ran a reception center in Santa Fe for newly arrived staff members on their way to Los Alamos.

directed to the same post office box address. Security guards picked them up for delivery in the camp. In some ways, the citizens of Los Alamos were almost prisoners—by their own choice—for as long as the war lasted. Except for the highest ranking people—and then only for special reasons—everyone was allowed only one outside visit a month.

The conditions encountered by each new arrival at the camp were in some ways like the pioneering towns of the Wild West. When Oppenheimer first came to Los Alamos in March 1943, he and Kitty had to stay in a hotel in Santa Fe for weeks until their apartment was ready. Three thousand army construction engineers raced to put up the necessary buildings: a main center and auditorium for meetings and recreation; five laboratories; a machine shop; storage buildings; barracks for military personnel; and apartments and dormitories for the civilians.

The buildings, whether for living quarters or for work, were flimsy and ramshackle. Even the apartments for the scientists and army officers were little more than shacks. The walls between apartments were so thin that residents could hear a neighbor sneeze. When the first arrivals came to camp, Los Alamos had no sewer system, no laundry, no garbage disposal, and only one telephone line.

These military style buildings served as homes for the technical staff at Los Alamos.

The streets in "the Hill," as the people of Los Alamos called it, were never paved. In wet weather, paths between buildings turned to ankle-deep mud. In dry weather, the town's residents had to fight dust. General Groves refused to pave the streets or have street lighting installed because he was determined to limit the project's costs.

As construction continued, though, life settled down. The people of Los Alamos, encouraged by their director, managed to create a lively social life. Many of the scientists and technicians played musical instruments and were able to organize an orchestra, a nineteen-piece band, and a choir. On week-

A car stuck in the mud of an unpaved street at Los Alamos.

ends, the residents went to square dances, parties, and movies. The women arranged for a school for the growing number of children. During the war years, 208 babies were born in Los Alamos. And on December 7, 1944, a daughter, Katherine—called Toni—was born to Robert and Kitty. Her birth certificate, like those of the other babies, listed the Santa Fe post box number as her birthplace.

Eventually, the citizens of Los Alamos elected a town council to help Oppenheimer run the city. Still, most problems, both scientific and social, ended up with "Oppie," as he was affectionately known. In almost all cases, he was able to work out differences of scientific opinions as well as social misunderstandings.

Living and working at the camp were never easy. The workday began at 7:30 A.M. and lasted well into the evening. Officially, everyone worked six days a week. Many of the scientists worked part of Sundays as well. At Los Alamos, Oppenheimer always opened his office before anyone else showed up for work.

Security was strict both inside and outside the camp. Married men could not discuss their work with their wives. Even Robert's wife Kitty, for example, had to show her pass to an army sentry to get into her own house. And the people in Santa Fe, who lived just thirty-five miles away, didn't learn what was going on until well after the war.

Rumors spread that Los Alamos was a poison gas factory, a plant for space ships, or a camp for antiwar protestors. To counter these rumors, Oppenheimer sent members of his staff into town with a different story. The army, they told Santa Fe's citizens, was making an "electric rocket." That became the official word. The real nature of the project, according to the high military command, was "the best kept secret of the war." That was what the U.S. government and the army wanted, and that was the way Oppenheimer managed it.

Despite the tension and stress, the isolation, the physical discomfort, and the hard work, morale stayed high, and no serious personal conflicts developed. No one quit; no one broke down. Perhaps the youthfulness of the people helped. Few were over forty, and most were in their twenties. They accepted the rough life as a kind of adventure—an adventure that held the excitement of working for a great cause, and the challenge of exploring new scientific territory. And, above all, their response was a reflection of and a tribute to their leader, Robert Oppenheimer.

Chapter/Nine

Building the Bomb

As the director of Los Alamos, a big part of Oppenheimer's job was to satisfy the pride and keep up the morale of the hundreds of scientists. Although they were all dedicated to the Manhattan Project, each of them was also, in a sense, an all-star player. Putting aside individual goals and achievement for the total team effort was not easy. "Oppie" managed to keep them reasonably happy, even though he was a tough and demanding boss.

Oppenheimer took part in the discussions and planning of each of the four main departments, keeping close watch on everyone's work. A story often told about his role at Los Alamos describes the time he came into a meeting room late one afternoon. A group of physicists had spent the whole day working out a problem. The blackboards were covered with complicated mathematical figures and equations that did not seem to make sense. The group was exhausted from their attempts to solve the problem and ready to try again the next day. Oppenheimer sat down and studied the blackboards for about fifteen minutes. Then he got up, made a few corrections on the blackboard, and left. This time, the equation worked.

Producing a successful bomb remained his major responsibility. Once a week, all four groups came together to report and discuss their progress, and to exchange ideas. Out of these discussions came the ideas for two kinds of nuclear weapons. The first of these would use uranium 235. At least thirty to forty pounds of U-235, one group estimated, would be needed for an effective chain reaction.

To trigger the atomic explosion in the uranium bomb, a shaped "lump" of U-235 would be shot like a bullet out of a gun at a second lump. When the two lumps collided, a chain reaction would be started, and the resulting fission would produce a nuclear blast. To make it happen, the uranium "bullet" would have to travel many times faster than an ordinary bullet.

After much checking, the scientists agreed that

Robert and Kitty Oppenheimer enjoyed social gatherings with the families of other scientists at Los Alamos.

this plan would work. The only problem at that point was collecting thirty to forty pounds of U-235. Many tons of raw uranium had to be processed to make one pound of U-235, and production was going so slowly that the staff faced the danger of losing the race against the Germans.

As a safeguard against a possible shortage, Oppenheimer authorized research to develop a different explosive system. This one would use plutonium, Pu-239, another highly radioactive metal. Just twelve to fifteen pounds of plutonium, the physicists calculated, would be required for a bomb. At this time, though, plutonium was only a theory in the minds of the physicists. A factory was built in Hanford, Washington, to produce it. A year later, in mid-1944, Los Alamos received its first delivery of Pu-239—one ounce of this dangerous material to use in experiments.

Still, because less material would be needed, the prospects for the plutonium bomb seemed more promising. Guided by the calculations of the Los Alamos staff, General Groves decided that by early 1945 there might be enough U-235 for one bomb, and enough Pu-239 for two. He ordered the scientific team to concentrate first on the plutonium bomb, without slowing down the effort to make the uranium weapon.

Oppenheimer had other technical and personal problems to deal with. Edward Teller had worked out a theory for a thermonuclear bomb. Instead of uranium as its basic element, it would use hydrogen and an isotope of hydrogen, deuterium. And instead of *fission*—splitting atoms to create an explosion—Teller's bomb would use *fusion*—forcing atoms together so suddenly and so tightly that they would break out in a violent "riot." That would produce an explosion many times more powerful than either the uranium or the plutonium bomb.

Teller had come to Los Alamos expecting to work on this particular project. Unfortunately for Teller, a fusion explosion had to be triggered first by a fission reaction, and there was still a shortage of material for that. Oppenheimer, pressured by General Groves, did not feel he could put Teller's nuclear device ahead of the other programs. This decision caused hard feelings between the two physicists. To satisfy Teller, Oppenheimer authorized him to set up a separate laboratory, and to organize his own group to work on nuclear fusion. As the months passed, the pressure to build the plutonium bomb increased. A major problem remained to be solved. To set off a nuclear explosion, the atoms had to be attacked from all sides at once. Yet the scientists believed that the "gun method" would not work for the plutonium bomb. It could not shoot the "bullet" at a high enough speed to trigger the chain reaction, and it could only hit the target from one direction. That wouldn't do the job.

Oppenheimer asked George Kistiakowsky, the Harvard professor of chemistry who had come to Los Alamos as an explosives expert, to find a different way to trigger a nuclear explosion. With Jim Tuck, a member of the British crew, Kistiakowsky created a clever system for aiming the shock waves given off by conventional explosives into the plutonium core. He designed these explosives to be shaped around the plutonium in what he called lenses, like the lenses of a camera. They would be spaced around the inside of a "hollow ball" in such a way that when the charge went off, each lens would focus, or aim, the force of the blast inward. The critical mass—the plutonium at its "boiling point"—would be hit from all directions at exactly the same time. This system, in theory, would produce the kind of nuclear explosion that Oppenheimer and his team needed.

By August 1944, Robert was able to assure General Groves that three bombs were on the way. Two would be uranium "gun" bombs, one more powerful than the other. And the third would be a plutonium bomb, even more powerful than the uranium devices. The crew nicknamed the uranium bomb Thin Man in honor of President Roosevelt. When a change in the gun mechanism made it possible to shorten the weapon, they changed the name to Little Boy. The plutonium bomb was called Fat Man because of its shape, and in honor of Winston Churchill.

The U-235 bomb, Oppenheimer told Groves, could be ready by August 1945. And if the new lens system tested out successfully, the plutonium bomb could be ready even sooner, by July 1945.

The Los Alamos team believed that the gun trigger on the uranium bombs would work. The team had less confidence in the lens system and argued that the plutonium bomb should be tested. General Groves opposed the idea of a test. If it succeeded, he feared that the scarce supply of Pu-239 would be used up or lost. If it failed, they would have to depend entirely on the uranium bomb. He worried that this would seriously delay the program, and the prospect of losing the race to the Germans haunted him.

Backed by his top scientists, Oppenheimer convinced Groves that a test was absolutely necessary. To quiet the general's fears about losing the plutonium, the team designed a bomb that would make it possible—they hoped—to contain the explosion inside a casing. Such a device would enable them to recover the plutonium.

They called the bomb built for this experiment Jumbo. The plutonium core would be enclosed by 5,300 pounds of high explosives, inside a container of solid concrete twenty-four inches thick. That assembly would rest inside a fifteen-inch-thick steel shell. Built in a steel mill in Ohio, the shell was shaped like a huge thermos bottle. It weighed more than 200 tons and was bigger than a railroad freight car.

Choosing a test site for Jumbo, and the other bombs, had begun long before. Oppenheimer led the search team, accompanied by Kenneth Bainbridge and two army majors. They looked for a flat stretch of land where the weather was favorable, where as few people as possible would have to be moved, and where they would be close enough to Los Alamos for convenient transportation.

The search team settled on a spot in the desert in the White Sands Missile Range, about 160 miles south of Los Alamos. The government already owned most of the land. Some of it was rented to cattle and sheep ranchers, but they could be moved without much trouble.

In keeping with military language, the point at which the bomb would be exploded was called

Workers move Jumbo on its way to the test site in the New Mexico desert.

"Ground Zero." Preparing Ground Zero was like building Los Alamos all over again, only much more complicated. Barracks, mess halls, kitchens, and store houses had to be built for the scientists and the army personnel would would operate the test.

To launch the bombs, two towers were erected. Bunkers were built so that people could observe the blasts without risking their lives. Made of earth and concrete, these shelters were positioned 5.7 miles from Ground Zero to the north, south, and west. Five hundred miles of wire were strung up on six-foot poles to connect the measuring instruments in the towers to those in the bunkers.

New roads had to be built, especially to support Jumbo. It traveled from Ohio to New Mexico very slowly on a specially designed railroad flatcar with a hollowed-out center. A canvas sheet covered it, and a heavily armed guard escorted it across the country. Jumbo finally arrived at Pope's Siding on the Santa Fe Railroad, twenty-five miles from Ground Zero. It crossed the final twenty-five miles on a specially built road.

Ground Zero was named Trinity Site, later shortened to just Trinity. There are many stories about how this name was chosen. Most of the Los Alamos staff credit the name to Oppenheimer. According to a widely accepted explanation of his choice, *Trinity* refers to the writings of the Hindu "bible." These scriptures, which Robert knew well, tell of the three natures of God: Brahma, the Creator; Vishnu, the preserver or caretaker of creation; and Shiva, the Destroyer. Hindus believe that nothing is ever completely destroyed. Whatever seems to be destroyed comes back in another form. Some of Robert's friends thought this is what he had in mind when he chose the name.

When Jumbo was finally in place, an argument started. Some of the scientists claimed that exploding the plutonium device inside Jumbo would wreck the instruments attached to it. Without this

Buildings at the Trinity test site.

information, the test would be useless. Oppenheimer decided to cancel the test and recover the plutonium.

Still, something had to be done with the huge "elephant," as General Groves called it. The army engineers built a seventy-foot tower a half-mile from Ground Zero. They placed Jumbo on a concrete slab in the tower and blew up the 5,300 pounds of dynamite. The explosion completely wrecked the tower, but Jumbo survived. Its huge, rusting shell still lies in the New Mexico desert.

By this time, Groves was really getting impatient. In February 1945, he ordered that no more

purely theoretical experiments be performed at Los
Alamos. The general demanded a July target date
for a final test. From now on, everyone would make
an all-out effort to put theory to work—to make
the real bomb.

Chapter/Ten

Sunrise at Trinity

Early in 1945, it became clear that Germany would lose the war. The Allies, led by General Dwight Eisenhower, had liberated France and were on the march. American intelligence had also discovered that, on Hitler's order, the Germans had stopped work on a nuclear bomb. They had put all their efforts into making V-2 rocket bombs that they used in a last, desperate effort to destroy Great Britain.

But even though there was no longer a threat of nuclear destruction from Germany, the war with Japan continued. Japanese forces were retreating, but fighting fiercely. On both sides, many soldiers were dying. The commanders of the American forces thought of the atomic bomb as a weapon that could possibly shorten the war. At Los Alamos, Groves and Oppenheimer kept up the pressure to finish the Manhattan Project.

Then, on April 12, 1945, President Franklin D. Roosevelt died suddenly in Warm Springs, Georgia. His death came as a shock to everyone, and especially to Robert Oppenheimer. President Roosevelt was the one who had ordered the development of the nuclear program. To Robert, the president's death was like an omen of failure. Robert had been working feverishly and had lost 30 pounds. On his six-foot, two-inch frame, his 110 pounds made him look like a walking skeleton. He became deeply depressed.

More than ever, Groves felt that the success of the Manhattan Project depended on Oppenheimer's leadership. He feared the director's depression would endanger the completion of the work. Ordering the FBI to ignore Frank Oppenheimer's membership in the Communist party, Groves arranged to have Robert's brother join him at Los Alamos. The general also brought Robert's friend, I. I. Rabi, from Chicago to help boost the director's spirits.

On May 7, 1945, Germany surrendered. The July target date for the bomb now became important for another reason. Harry S. Truman, Roosevelt's vice-president, had succeeded to the presidency. In mid-July, the new U.S. president was scheduled to meet in Potsdam, Germany, with Winston Churchill, the British prime minister, and with Joseph Stalin, the Soviet leader. The purpose of the meeting was to discuss the future of Europe, and to plan for the end of the war with Japan.

The American military chiefs wanted the test carried out before, or during, the meeting to make sure the bomb would work. That would give President Truman a stronger position in dealing with the Soviets. On June 9, responding to General Groves's urging, Oppenheimer sent out the following order to all key Los Alamos personnel: "Trinity must not delay the test of the gadget [the bomb], and we must schedule operations at the earliest possible date—July 4, 1945." However, because the lens moldings for the plutonium bomb and other engineering problems were still causing difficulties, Robert persuaded the general to agree to a short postponement—to Monday, July 16, at 4:00 A.M.

Enough plutonium would be ready for at least two, and probably three, weapons. The first test, then, would use a plutonium Fat Man. The bomb was egg-shaped, more than twelve feet long and five feet across, and weighed about five tons.

The engineers had designed the plutonium nuclear core to be assembled separately and inserted into the middle of the conventional explosives at the last possible minute. They did this to lessen the chances of an accidental blowup. The parts of the core came together in a special way, like a puzzle made of cubes and solid rectangles of metal. The lenses to control the inward force of the blast had to be carefully machined and polished, because every piece had to fit exactly.

Now the movement of materials from Los Alamos to Trinity began in earnest. Security was tighter than ever. Everyone—scientists, engineers, soldiers—had to carry a special pass. Only one stop was approved on the six-hour run: a café in the town of Belen. The chef in the café was supposed to be a government agent, stationed there by General Groves to make sure no one breached security, or even made a phone call.

On Thursday, July 12, the separate parts of the plutonium core were put into two specially built suitcases. These were placed on the back seat of Robert Bacher's sedan, where one of Oppenheimer's students, Philip Morrison, sat holding them. A three-car convoy—one military vehicle in front of the sedan and one behind—drove the "hot" package down to an old ranch house near Trinity.

At midnight of the same day, a much bigger convoy drove out of Los Alamos for Trinity. It

Los Alamos staff members carry the core of the atomic bomb from Robert Bacher's sedan into the MacDonald ranch house.

carried the bomb minus the core. The run between the two camps had been practiced many times with dummy bombs of the same size and weight, to see how well they would stand up on the rough roads. Although the trip was supposed to be top secret, the convoy went through every town on the way with red lights flashing and sirens shrieking. It was a strange way to keep a secret.

Oppenheimer followed the convoy the next day. The details of the Trinity test were now in the hands of the specialists. Still, Robert was everywhere, nervously going from place to place, puffing and chewing on his pipe, checking every move.

At the Trinity test site, a 100-foot steel tower had been built at Ground Zero. The plan was to explode the bomb from the top of the tower rather than drop it from an airplane. This, too, was a safety measure. But a B-29 bomber would fly over the tower just before the blast to practice an actual air drop—to prepare for dropping a real bomb in a wartime situation.

On Saturday afternoon, July 14, final assembly began. At the base of the tower, Kistiakowsky's crew prepared the bomb to receive the plutonium core. Another team brought the core, not yet fitted together, from the nearby ranch house. They carried it very carefully on a stretcher.

At the base of the tower at Ground Zero, staff workers unload the bomb before completing the assembly by placing the core in it.

The parts had to be joined together with extreme care to keep the plutonium from going "critical" and starting a chain reaction too soon. If this happened, the crew would be exposed to a deadly dose of radioactive poisoning. Geiger counters monitored every step. In the silence in which the men worked, the clicking of the Geigers was like the beating of drums.

When the core was assembled, a small crane hoisted it above the bomb and then slowly lowered it into its "nest." As the core descended, the Geiger counters grew louder, the clicking faster. The men stopped the crane to slow down the reaction. Then, just when the core was supposed to slip tightly into its "bed," it stuck. It would not fit.

In every rehearsal, dummy models had never failed to slip in snugly. Yet this was the first time the core contained live plutonium. Robert Bacher had an idea. He put on some heavy rubber gloves and felt the core. It was very hot; the heat had expanded the metal just enough to prevent a fit. The crew decided to wait to see if the core would cool off. It did, and slipped neatly into place. Everyone sighed with relief.

Now the crew began lifting the bomb, by pulleys and tracks, to the iron shack at the top of the tower. Kistiakowsky and Oppenheimer stayed to help winch it up. The crew spent two hours hoisting the bomb up the platform.

With the bomb in place, much work still remained to be done. Someone had to connect the sixty-four detonators (triggers) to the bomb, and to the controls and measuring instruments at the three observation bunkers. Two other crew members had to adjust the timing mechanism that would set off the detonators, by remote control, after the area had been cleared. Preparations continued all day Saturday and into Sunday. The network of wires around the bomb looked like a huge bowl of steel spaghetti.

The bomb, completely assembled, rests on top of the 100-foot steel tower.

Once the bomb was assembled, the military guard retreated to the bunkers. General Groves continued to worry about sabotage. To satisfy him, several scientists and a few army officers spent the night at the tower with flashlights and one machine gun.

On Sunday afternoon, Oppenheimer climbed the tower, alone, for a last check, even though there was nothing more he could do. It had begun to storm. Strong winds blew, rattling the iron shack, and causing the tower to sway. Alone with his thoughts, Robert seemed to hear nothing.

Jack Holland, who headed a team of weather forecasters, had predicted a clear early Monday morning. Yet on Sunday evening, the storm grew worse. Although the tower had been protected with safety devices against lightning, a lightning bolt actually hit and blew up one of the devices. It looked as if the test would have to be postponed. Both Groves and Oppenheimer were angry with Holland, and they decided to hold a last-minute meeting with him to make a final decision. If the wind stayed as it was at midnight, it would pour down a flood of radioactive dust on the north shelter.

Several thousand army troops waited at the three shelters to witness the blast. On Sunday night, busloads of government officials and staff people from Los Alamos joined them. They included Edward Teller, Hans Bethe, Ernest Lawrence, and one reporter, William Laurence, from the *New York Times*. All of them waited through the stormy night.

At two in the morning, the storm still raged. Oppenheimer waited for Holland to arrive at Trinity Base Camp. General Groves and two of his aides came in immediately after Holland, along with three more meteorologists. "What in hell is wrong with the weather?" Groves shouted, as if Holland was responsible for the storm.

The four o'clock blastoff was impossible, Holland said. Could it be delayed until nine? Oppenheimer said yes, but the general wouldn't hear of it. The weather forecasters studied their charts and made some phone calls. They decided there might be a break in the storm between five and six.

"Okay," the general said, "we'll go at 5:30 for sure." And to Holland he added, "You better be right on this or I'll hang you." He also phoned the governor of New Mexico, John Dempsey, at 3:00 A.M. Groves told the governor that he might have to declare martial law and take command of the state's government in order to have his troops lead the population out of the region. He did not explain why to the governor.

Holland and Oppenheimer left immediately for the south shelter. At the tower, Kenneth Bainbridge waited for last-minute instructions. At 4:40 Holland signaled okay on the weather, and Oppenheimer phoned Bainbridge to set the timing mechanism for a 5:30 explosion. Weather conditions would not be perfect, but at least the wind direction was right.

With Bainbridge at the tower were Kistiakowsky and two other crew members. They set the relays, turned on the switches, and drove off at 5:05. They would have less than twenty-five minutes to get to the south shelter. If their car broke down, they would have to run almost six miles in those twenty-five minutes. That would be faster than any champion runner had ever done it.

The countdown began. At 5:25, a rocket signaled a first warning. Then two more rockets went off at 5:28 and 5:29. At T-minus forty-five seconds, Joe McKibbin, who had been with Bainbridge at the tower, threw the last switch from the south shelter. As the final seconds passed, a civilian radio station not far away broadcast on the same frequency, playing a recording of Tchaikovsky's *Nutcracker Suite*. Everyone at all three shelters could hear the music.

A few seconds before 5:30 A.M. on Monday, July 16, 1945, the first atomic bomb exploded. For the people who witnessed the explosion, it seemed as if the sun appeared suddenly out of total darkness at high noon. People in three states saw the flash. The instruments measured the heat as equal to the heat of the sun, and the light as equal to twenty suns.

An old man, many miles away, said later: "The sun came up in the west, and in a few minutes went down again in the west." Georgia Green, a university student, had an even more startling experience. Her brother-in-law was driving her to the University of New Mexico in Albuquerque. They were about seventy-five miles north of Ground Zero when the bomb exploded. She jumped in her seat. "What was that?" she cried. Georgia Green had been totally blind from birth. For the first time in her life, she was able to tell light from darkness.

Only one newspaper story appeared, and only in New Mexico. The army explained the incident as an accidental explosion of a warehouse full of ammunition, with no loss of human life.

Shortly after the explosion, General Groves sent a telegram to Secretary of War Stimson, who was in Potsdam with President Truman. The telegram read: "Operated this morning. Diagnosis not yet complete but results seem satisfactory and already exceed expectations. . . .Dr. Groves pleased. . . ."

0.006 SEC.
N

100 METERS

0.016 SEC.
N

100 METERS

0.053 SEC.

100 METERS

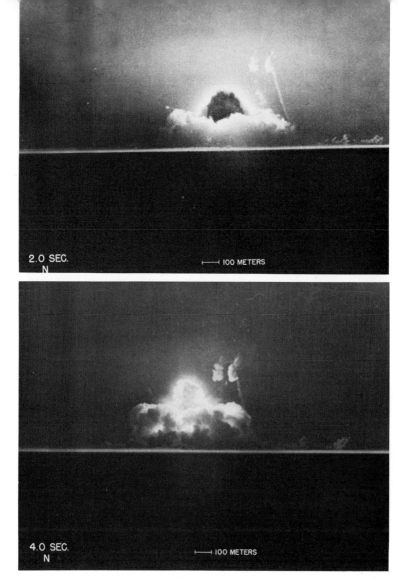

2.0 SEC.
N
⊢———⊣ 100 METERS

4.0 SEC.
N
⊢———⊣ 100 METERS

These photographs of the Trinity test explosion show a sequence of views ranging from .006 seconds (top, left hand page) to 4.0 seconds after the explosion (bottom, right hand page).

At the south bunker, George Kistiakowsky, covered with mud, hugged Robert Oppenheimer in an outburst of joy. The master of explosives had bet the director a month's salary against ten dollars that the test would succeed. Overcome with emotion, all the director could think of was the bet. "I haven't got ten dollars with me," he said. "I'll pay you later." The Los Alamos staff people joined hands and did a chain dance of victory around their leader.

When the excitement and triumph had calmed down a little, Oppenheimer said, "My faith in the human mind has been somewhat restored." At first, he was happy and relieved that the project had succeeded. Yet later that day, he would quote the Hindu bible again with one of his most famous sayings: "I am become Death, the Destroyer of worlds." This was Robert's way of expressing a growing fear about this remarkable scientific achievement. It was a fear for the terrible harm human beings might cause if they did not properly control this new and enormously powerful weapon of destruction.

Oppenheimer and General Groves examine the twisted remains of the tower at Ground Zero after the atomic test explosion.

Chapter/Eleven

A Strange Justice

When the atomic bomb exploded at Trinity, the war with Germany had been over for two months, but the war against Japan continued. Clearly, Japan was losing. The U.S. Navy and the Marines had driven the Japanese back from their bases in the Pacific Ocean. The American forces were close enough to send squadrons of B-29 bombers to attack the Japanese mainland. U.S. planes had fire-bombed the capital city of Tokyo more than once. Still, the Japanese refused to give up.

President Harry Truman had to decide whether or not to drop an atomic bomb on that country. Some government officials and army officers argued that Japan could be defeated without the bomb. Others pointed to the Japanese "kamikaze" attitude: suicide before surrender. If the Japanese fought to the death, this argument went, too many lives would be lost in an invasion—Japanese as well as American. An atomic bomb, then, would result in fewer lives lost than an invasion.

Several scientists proposed that top Japanese leaders be invited to a test explosion in the Pacific Ocean, much like the one at Trinity. These scientists believed that seeing the atomic explosion might scare the Japanese into surrendering. Oppenheimer and his chief assistants took part in these discussions, but the final decision rested with President Truman.

Oppenheimer argued against a demonstration. He believed that such a test might make the Japanese more determined to fight on, especially if the bomb failed to explode. The element of surprise, he insisted, was important. In the end, after the Japanese ignored a general warning to surrender, President Truman gave the order to drop an atomic bomb.

Kyoto, a historical city rich in the culture of ancient Japan, was the first choice as a target. Oppenheimer, however, insisted that the attack should be strictly military in nature. Because of his objections, Hiroshima, an important army depot, replaced Kyoto as first choice.

A team of experts from Los Alamos had flown

The "Little Boy" bomb that destroyed the city of Hiroshima, Japan, looked much like this later atomic bomb.

to the Pacific island of Tinian to prepare for the mission. Late on the evening of August 5, they assembled and armed the Little Boy uranium bomb. Long before dawn the next morning, the crew of a B-29 bomber, the *Enola Gay*, took off. At 9:14 A.M. on August 6, 1945, the bombardier released Little Boy over Hiroshima.

The bomb completely destroyed two-thirds of the city. More than 80,000 persons died instantly, and half that many were missing. Thousands more suffered terrible radiation burns and sickness.

Three days later, another B-29, *Bock's Car*, dropped a Fat Man plutonium bomb on Nagasaki.

Hiroshima, Japan, in September 1945, about a month after a U.S. B-29 bomber dropped an atomic bomb on the city. The building at the center of the picture became a monument after World War II.

Half the city was destroyed, and more than 100,000 people were killed or injured. Among them were two American prisoners of war who had been moved to a camp near Nagasaki just two weeks before. Another plutonium bomb was prepared on Tinian for a third drop. On August 14, before the United States could use this bomb, Japan surrendered unconditionally.

The end of the war was a time of celebration for all Americans and for people the world over. It was also a time of great joy for the staff at Los Alamos, because of their tremendous contribution in speeding up the end of the struggle. Their project had been a great success. And yet, they also experienced a letdown. The loss of life and the awful damage caused by the bombs saddened everyone.

Late in August, Oppenheimer was able to get away for a few days with Kitty and their two children, Peter and Toni. It was the family's first vacation in three years. They spent the time at their beloved Perro Caliente ranch. Here, Robert began to plan his future.

Tremendous new developments in nuclear science, both for military and civilian purposes, were now within reach. The work at Los Alamos would go on for some time. As the leader of the history-making Los Alamos project, Oppenheimer fully ex-

Kitty Oppenheimer enjoys a happy moment with Toni and Peter.

pected to play a part in the advances in this new field. After much thought, he decided he could contribute most by returning to teaching. He accepted a position at the California Institute of Technology.

Robert Oppenheimer resigned as director of Los Alamos, effective October 16, 1945. At that time he recommended that the laboratory be kept going for weapons research and for making some bomb parts. Robert helped General Groves choose Norris Bradbury, a physicist, to succeed him as director.

On October 16, the entire staff of Los Alamos gathered for a retirement ceremony to honor their leader. General Groves presented him with a certificate of gratitude from the U.S. government. The ceremony came as a surprise to Oppenheimer. Expressing his thanks, he spoke briefly of atomic bombs as a possible "curse," but also, he hoped, as "an instrument that would unite the world in law and humanity."

The award from the government was the first of many he would receive. The city of Berkeley and the university honored him. *Time* magazine featured him in a cover story that called him "the father of the atomic bomb."

Oppenheimer gave most of the credit to his colleagues. Yet even some of his critics said that if he

General Groves presents a certificate of gratitude from the U.S. government to Robert Oppenheimer to honor his contribution to the success of the Manhattan Project.

had done nothing more than recruit and organize the "eggheads"—the scientists who built the bomb—he would have done his country a great service. But he did much more. Under extremely difficult conditions, he led a team of 1,500 people to success in one of history's greatest scientific accomplishments.

He taught for a year at Caltech, and then, a year later, the Institute for Advanced Studies at Princeton University named him to succeed Albert Einstein as its director. He did not, however, devote himself only to teaching. The whole field of atomic and nuclear energy was growing swiftly. When a number of government agencies called upon him for his advice and services, he responded enthusiastically. At the same time that he assumed his position at Princeton, he became chairperson of the General Advisory Committee of the U.S. Atomic Energy Commission (AEC).

The AEC planned and regulated the use of nuclear energy in power plants for the production of electricity. It also cooperated with the armed services in atomic weapons research for military use. Oppenheimer had a role in several organizations that dealt with these matters. Since much of his work continued to be highly secret, he had to go through another security check to make sure that he was a completely trustworthy and loyal citizen. He passed this test with ease.

And then, on August 29, 1949, the Soviet Union exploded its first atomic bomb. This test did not completely surprise American physicists. They all agreed that sooner or later, other nations with strong research programs and the necessary materials would be able to make such a bomb. Still, the test did come as a shock to the U.S. government. Neither the government nor the scientists expected the Soviets to build a successful bomb for at least five or, more likely, ten years.

Both the government and the military wanted

to keep the news of the Soviet success from the American people. Oppenheimer, who was as surprised as everyone by that early success, now argued that the time for secrecy was over. He pleaded, as a member of the AEC, to make the whole subject of atomic energy as understandable as possible to all Americans, and to people around the world. He proposed that an international body be set up to control the development of nuclear science for both civilian and military use. All the leading nations of the world, including the Soviet Union, would be invited to become members of this organization.

During World War II, the Soviets had complained about not getting enough technical help from the Allies while Soviet forces were fighting desperately against the invading German army. Many in the scientific community believed that atomic knowledge should be shared with the Soviets. The U.S. government and the military said no. They were suspicious of that nation's postwar plans, and wanted to keep the advantage on the American side. In fact, President Truman did not tell Stalin about the U.S. atomic bomb test until eight days after the Potsdam Conference had begun.

As the war ended, the Soviets took control of several Eastern European countries and closed them off behind what Winston Churchill called the "Iron

Curtain." American suspicions were confirmed. A new wave of anti-Soviet feeling rose up in the United States. And when that Communist country exploded its first atomic bomb, the fear of communism increased.

Investigations now began to uncover how the Soviet Union was able to develop a bomb so quickly. FBI agents arrested Klaus Fuchs, an English physicist who had come to Los Alamos with the British mission. The FBI accused him of giving the Soviets great amounts of detailed technical information, and he confessed to being a Soviet spy.

Fuchs had delivered this critical information through David Greenglass, an American soldier whose unit was stationed at Los Alamos. Greenglass had passed the material on to his sister and brother-in-law, Ethel and Julius Rosenberg, who were members of the American Communist party. They were arrested, tried for treason, found guilty, and executed as spies.

No one ever accused Oppenheimer of being in any way connected with this spy ring, or involved in any leak of classified information. Yet during the war years, he had openly proposed that the Soviets be informed—without sharing any scientific secrets—about the project to develop the bomb at Los Alamos. In the new anti-Soviet atmosphere, his past actions, along with his suggestion for an international body to control nuclear research, seemed suspicious.

Oppenheimer's friendships with known Communists in the 1930s, and his support for some of their causes, now came back to haunt him. It is possible that these stories were revived by a few people who disliked him, who resented his brilliance, or who were jealous of his fame.

The FBI revived an incident involving his old friend, Professor Haakon Chevalier. An English engineer, George Eltenton, who had worked for an oil company in California, had met and become friendly with Chevalier. The Englishman had lived and worked in the Soviet Union. According to the FBI, he had told Chevalier that he knew about Oppenheimer's work, and that he could deliver technical information to the Soviets.

It was not clear that Eltenton had actually asked Chevalier to approach Oppenheimer with such a plan. But the French professor did discuss it with his friend at Robert's home before the physicist moved to Los Alamos. Oppenheimer himself reported the incident to the security officer. Yet for a long time, he tried to keep Chevalier's name a secret. That, too, may have been a mistake.

The old quarrel with Edward Teller at Los Alamos came up again. After the war, Teller had finally succeeded in making a hydrogen bomb. But when news of the Soviet success broke, Teller accused his colleague of "not being enthusiastic enough" about the hydrogen bomb, and thus delaying its development. In effect, he hinted that Oppenheimer was not a patriotic American.

In the postwar years, many scientists began to worry about the possible destruction of the world in a nuclear conflict. They campaigned for strict control over weapons development. Since Oppenheimer agreed with this viewpoint, many people thought his stand on the issue also reflected a lack of patriotism. As the most prominent of the nuclear physicists, he received more than his share of blame for what many people interpreted as an antinuclear attitude.

In the growing anti-Soviet, anti-Communist mood of the country, an increasing number of people said the great scientist was not to be trusted. On December 23, 1953, the Atomic Energy Commission temporarily suspended his security clearance, pending a hearing.

The AEC began hearing the case in April 1954. It was not actually a trial as in a court of law, but it did have a "prosecutor," a "defense attorney," and many witnesses. Oppenheimer himself testified at

Edward Teller spoke out against Robert Oppenheimer during the Atomic Energy Commission hearings.

length. Although he refused to talk about his brother Frank and Frank's membership in the Communist party, on all other issues he was completely open and honest. He explained carefully that, from 1939 on, he no longer had any sympathies for the Communists or any of their ideas. During the war, he said, he was concerned only with an American victory.

Many of his colleagues—I. I. Rabi, Hans Bethe, as well as General Groves—testified in his favor. They called him a dedicated and loyal American. Chevalier and Eltenton both testified that the director of Los Alamos had flatly refused to have anything to do with a scheme to deliver nuclear secrets to the Soviets. However, different and conflicting versions of this story left some doubts about what really happened.

Others testified against him. The prosecutor focused on his supposed opposition to the hydrogen bomb. Teller admitted that "I have always assumed, and I assume now that he is loyal to the United States." Still, he argued that his fellow physicist was too "hung up" on his own opinions to be trusted with authority in such critical matters as nuclear policy. Teller's testimony did some damage to Oppenheimer, but it also cost Teller the friendship of a great many other scientists.

The hearing lasted almost four weeks. During this time, the commission did not accuse Oppenheimer of wrongdoing or disloyalty. In fact, the FBI, which had kept a careful watch on the director during the war, had no evidence that he even leaked information carelessly. Despite the lack of evidence against him, on June 29, 1954, the AEC voted four to one not to give back his security clearance.

For Robert Oppenheimer, the AEC's decision was a heavy blow. It was as if the coach, the team captain, and the star player were being dismissed from the national team because he could not be trusted. The man who, according to General Groves and President Truman, had led the country to its greatest scientific achievement, was told he had nothing more to offer. The AEC had added a strange and sad twist to a remarkable career.

The verdict affected Oppenheimer's family deeply. Kitty, who had always had a drinking problem, now began to drink more. Their son Peter, who adored his father, was especially bitter. A shy teenager, he felt that the country had done a great injustice to his father. Peter's bitterness may have caused him to do poorly at school, to his father's great distress.

Although Robert's work had always come first, he tried to spend more time with his children. He was not entirely successful in this effort, and his high expectations for Peter caused conflicts between father and son. Apparently trying to escape the hurt he felt, he began to travel around the world, always in connection with his teaching. What bothered him most was not a feeling that he had done something wrong, but that his personality and pride had offended some people. He blamed himself for that. Under the burden of his family's sorrows and his own self-doubts, he aged rapidly.

And yet, most of his old friends rallied to his side. In October 1954, the Institute for Advanced Studies at Princeton reappointed him as director. Since he had not been charged with breaking a law, he was free to go on teaching. He lectured about nuclear science and about the social problems it posed in the United States, Europe, and South America. Audiences everywhere greeted him with standing ovations.

Eventually, Oppenheimer's travels made him a gentler, more humble person. His son Peter discovered a more open kindness in his father, and they grew closer. Robert's public image also changed. Still, despite growing sentiment in the scientific community against the unfairness of the AEC's decision, the commission was not persuaded to change its ruling on his security clearance. This

Robert Oppenheimer after the Atomic Energy Commission hearings.

wave of sentiment, however, did build pressure to remedy a harsh action that more and more people saw as an injustice.

In 1955, the AEC established the Enrico Fermi Award. Along with a certificate, it included a gold medal and a check from the U.S. government for $50,000. The award honored "outstanding contributions to the development, use, or control of atomic energy." In 1963, at the urging of many scientists, including Edward Teller, the AEC voted unanimously to give the award to Robert Oppenheimer. The commission made the announcement on November 22, and planned to have President John F. Kennedy make the presentation two weeks later. Later on that same day, President Kennedy was assassinated.

Nevertheless, the ceremony was held. On December 2, 1963, the new president, Lyndon B. Johnson, presented the honors. It was a moment of justice for a great and distinguished man. After some moments of silence, he turned to the president and said, "I think it is just possible, Mr. President, that it has taken some charity and courage for you to make this award today. That would seem to be a good augury for all our futures."

Despite increasing physical frailty, Robert continued to teach. He had hoped to write a history of

*On December 2, 1963, Robert Oppenheimer receives the Enrico Fermi
Award from President Lyndon B. Johnson.*

modern physics, but he became ill in 1966. The doctors found that he had cancer of the throat. On February 18, 1967, at the age of 62, Robert Oppenheimer died at his home in Princeton, New Jersey. Hundreds of friends, famous scientists, and top government officials, led by General Leslie Groves, came to honor him at a memorial service at Princeton University. They praised him as a great scientist, as a statesman, and as a teacher and inspiration for the generation of physicists who followed him.

After the service, Kitty took his ashes to the Virgin Islands in the Caribbean Sea. Perhaps as a symbol of his love of sailing, she—with a few special friends—scattered the ashes in the sea.

Robert Oppenheimer's mission was finished.

/ Afterword

The explosion of the first atomic bomb on that Monday morning in July 1945 was more than a successful scientific achievement, and more than a way to end a war. It marked—for better or worse— the dawn of the atomic age. For the first time in history, human beings could control a force as powerful as anything in nature. It was, and is, a force that could destroy the planet Earth and all forms of life on it.

Many problems have developed as a result of this discovery. The creation of an atomic bomb has led to an arms race between the two great world powers, the United States and the Soviet Union. Each nation has huge stockpiles of nuclear weapons. Some military leaders say that the fear of destruc-

tion caused by these weapons has prevented a world
war since 1945. Yet no one knows what might happen if the regional wars that still occur around the
world begin to spread. That fear may be one reason
the governments of the United States and the Soviet
Union are trying to establish treaties to reduce the
number of nuclear weapons.

After World War II, the U.S. government encouraged scientists to develop peaceful uses for
nuclear energy, and they accepted the challenge
with great enthusiasm. Nuclear-generated electricity
promised a cheaper power that would never run
out, unlike the limited supplies of oil, coal, and
natural gas. But accidents in nuclear-generating
plants in both the Soviet Union and the United
States have raised disturbing questions. And no one
has yet proposed a completely safe way to dispose
of the radioactive waste materials produced by gen-
erating electricity from nuclear fission.

The question of how nations would use this
newfound power troubled Robert Oppenheimer
throughout the remaining years of his life. Oppenheimer warned that if nuclear energy became,
first and foremost, a military weapon, people
might someday "curse the name of Los Alamos."
This issue bothered many other scientists who had
helped him make the project a success, and it con-

tinues to bother them and their successors today.

Still, like many scientific challenges, the making of the atomic bomb seemed destined to happen. In a speech marking the fortieth anniversary of Los Alamos in 1983, Robert's friend I. I. Rabi summed up the feelings of most of the surviving pioneers and the scientists who followed them. "What we did," he said, "was inevitable. What we did was fortunate for the United States and for the world— as of that time." Rabi might have also said that if the Nazis had been first with the bomb, it would have changed the course of modern world history. And if the Los Alamos project was necessary, some- one had to lead the way. That person was Robert Oppenheimer.

Could someone else have accomplished what he did? Possibly, but he was the one chosen, and he came through. He helped the United States win a great victory, as much in science as in war. For that, he continues to be honored today by scientists everywhere—not only for his genius in theoretical physics, but also for his ability to bring the theories and ideas of others into a working harmony.

Whether atomic energy is directed toward war or toward peace, many problems still need to be solved. Robert Oppenheimer deserves neither all the praise for opening the door to the atomic age,

nor all the blame for its possible terrible conse-
quences. What happens to this awesome power will
depend on how nations use it.

   If they use it wisely, it will be another tribute to
Robert Oppenheimer, the man and the scientist.

Appendix

Major Events in Oppenheimer's Life

1904   J. Robert Oppenheimer born April 22 in New York City

1912   Brother, Frank Oppenheimer, born August 12

1921   Oppenheimer graduates from Ethical Culture School

1925   Oppenheimer graduates from Harvard University with top honors

1926-27   Two years of graduate study at Cambridge University in England, and University of Gottingën in Germany

1927   Oppenheimer receives Ph.D. in physics from the University of Gottingën

1928-29   Research fellow at University of Leiden in the Netherlands and Technical Institute in Switzerland

1929   Oppenheimer appointed to a teaching position in the physics departments at both the University of California at Berkeley and the California Institute of Technology (Caltech) at Pasadena

1940   Oppenheimer marries Katherine Puening Harrison

1941   Son, Peter, born May 12

1941   United States enters World War II against Japan and Germany following Japanese attack on Pearl Harbor

1942   U.S. government chooses Oppenheimer to be coordinator of atomic research at the Office of Scientific Research and Development

1942   General Leslie R. Groves chooses Oppenheimer to be director of the Manhattan Project at Los Alamos, New Mexico

1944	Daughter, Katherine, born December 7
1945	First atomic bomb exploded near Alamogordo, New Mexico, July 16, at the Trinity test site
1945	U.S. bombers drop atomic bombs on the Japanese cities of Hiroshima (August 6) and Nagasaki (August 9); Japan surrenders August 14
1945	Oppenheimer resigns as director of Los Alamos in October, and resumes teaching at Caltech
1947	Oppenheimer is appointed as director of the Institute of Advanced Study at Princeton University in New Jersey; also appointed chairperson of the General Advisory Committee of the U.S. Atomic Energy Commission (AEC)
1953	AEC suspends Oppenheimer's security clearance pending a hearing and review of his past political activities
1954	Following the four-week hearing, the AEC votes not to restore Oppenheimer's security clearance; he is barred from all government work in physics

1963   U.S. government honors Oppenheimer on December 2 with the Enrico Fermi Award for his outstanding contributions to the science of physics

1967   Oppenheimer dies on February 18 in Princeton, New Jersey; his ashes are buried at sea

Selected Bibliography

Brown, Anthony Cace and MacDonald, Charles B.
  The Secret History of the Atomic Bomb. New York:
  G. P. Putnam and Sons, 1976.
Bush, Vannevar. *Modern Arms and Free Men.* New
  York: Simon and Schuster, 1949.
Calder, Nigil. *Nuclear Nightmares.* New York: Viking
  Press, 1979.
Chevalier, Haakon. *Oppenheimer: The Story of a
  Friendship.* New York: George Braziller, 1965.
Davis, Nuel Pharr. *Lawrence and Oppenheimer.* New
  York: Simon and Schuster, 1965.
Goodchild, Peter. *J. Robert Oppenheimer: Shatterer of
  Worlds.* New York: Fromm International, 1985.
Groves, Leslie R. *Now It Can Be Told.* New York:
  Harper and Row, 1962.

Hersey, John. *Hiroshima*. New York: Alfred A. Knopf, 1946.

Jungh, Robert. *Brighter Than a Thousand Suns*. New York: Harcourt, Brace, Jovanovich, 1958.

Kunetka, James W. *Oppenheimer: The Years of Risk*. Englewood Cliffs, NJ: Prentice-Hall, 1982.

Lamont, Lansing. *Days of Trinity*. New York: Atheneum, 1965.

Laurence, William L. *Dawn Over Zero*. New York: Alfred A. Knopf, 1951.

Oppenheimer, J. Robert. *The Open Mind*. New York: Simon and Schuster, 1955.

Royal, Denise. *The Story of J. R. Oppenheimer*. New York: St. Martin's Press, 1969.

Smith, Alice Kimball and Weiner, Charles. *Robert Oppenheimer: Letters and Recollections*. Cambridge, MA: Harvard University Press, 1980.

Szasz, Ferenc Morton. *The Day the Sun Rose Twice*. Albuquerque, NM: University of New Mexico Press, 1984.

Index